Caldecott & Co.

Caldecott & Co.

NOTES ON BOOKS & PICTURES

Maurice Sendak

The Noonday Press

Michael di Capua Books

Farrar, Straus and Giroux

For Ursula Nordstrom

Contents

One

The Shape of Music

Vivify, *quicken*, and *vitalize*—of these three
synonyms, *quicken*, I think, best suggests the genuine
spirit of animation, the breathing to life, the swing
into action, that I consider an essential quality in pictures for children's books. *To quicken* means, for the
illustrator, the task first of comprehending the nature
of his text and then of giving life to that comprehension in his own medium, the picture.

The conventional techniques of graphic animation
are related to this intention only in that they provide
an instrument with which the artist can begin his
work. Sequential scenes that tell a story in pictures, as
in the comic strip, are an example of one form of
animation. It is no difficult matter for an artist to simu-
late action, but it is something else to *quicken*, to
create an inner life that draws breath from the artist's
deepest perception.

The word *quicken* has other, more subjective associa-
tions for me. It suggests something musical, something
rhythmic and impulsive. It suggests a beat—a heart-
beat, a musical beat, the beginning of a dance. This
association proclaims music as one source from which
my own pictures take life. For me, "to conceive musi-

cally" means to quicken the life of the illustrated book. All of my pictures are created against a background of music. More often than not, my instinctive choice of composer or musical form for the day has the galvanizing effect of making me conscious of my direction. I find something uncanny in the way a musical phrase, a sensuous vocal line, or a patch of Wagnerian color will clarify an entire approach or style for a new work. A favorite occupation of mine, some years back, was sitting in front of the record player as though possessed by a dybbuk, and allowing the music to provoke an automatic, stream-of-consciousness kind of drawing. Sometimes the pictures that resulted were merely choreographed episodes, imagined figures dancing imagined ballets. More interesting to me, and much more useful for my work, are the childhood fantasies that were reactivated by the music and explored uninhibitedly by the pen.

Music's peculiar power of releasing fantasy has always fascinated me. An inseparable part of my memories of childhood, music was the inevitable, animating accompaniment to the make-believe. No childhood fantasy of mine was complete without the restless, ceaseless sound of impromptu humming, the din of unconscious music-making that conjured up just the right fantastical atmosphere. All children seem to know what the mysterious, the riding-fiercely-across-the-plains (accompanied by hearty, staccato thigh slaps), and the plaintive conventionally sound like; and I have no doubt that this kind of musical contribution enriches each particular fantasy. The spontaneous breaking into song and dance seems so natural and instinctive a part of childhood. It is perhaps the medium through which children best express the inexpressible; fantasy and feeling lie deeper than words —beyond the words yet available to a child—and both demand a more profound, more biological expression, the primitive expression of music. Recently I watched a mother tell her little boy a familiar, ritualistic story while he embellished the tale with an original hummed score. He kept up a swinging motion "in time" to the story, then punctuated the end with a series of sharp, imitation bugle sounds and a wild jungle jump.

My intention is not to prove music the sole enlivening force behind the creation of pictures for children. But music is the impulse that most stimulates my own work and I invariably sense a musical element in the work of the artists I admire, those artists who achieve the authentic liveliness that is the essence of the picture book, a movement that is never still, and that children, I am convinced, recognize and enjoy as something familiar to themselves.

Maurice Boutet de Monvel's illustrations for La Fontaine *(Fables choisies pour les enfants)* exemplify this quality of authentic liveliness. His exquisitely animated pictures have, to an astonishing degree, an inner life of their own. Every aspect of individual character and gesture seems to have been explored, and the result is a synthesis of movement that is a triumph of animation. The continuous flow across each page is comparable to a sustained and shaded melodic line.

The lamb in Boutet de Monvel's delicate rendering of "Le Loup et l'agneau" performs, before meeting an unjust fate, a sequence of linear arabesques, a dance of death that painfully conveys and dramatically enlarges the fable's grim meaning. The eye follows from picture to picture the swift development of the story—the fatalistic "folding up," the quiet inevitability of the lamb's movements, ending in a dying-swan gesture of hopeless resignation. And then the

LE LOUP ET L'AGNEAU

La raison du plus fort est toujours la meilleure :
Nous l'allons montrer tout à l'heure.

Un agneau se désaltérait
Dans le courant d'une onde pure.

Un loup survient à jeun, qui cherchait aventure,
Et que la faim en ces lieux attirait.

« Qui te rend si hardi de troubler mon breuvage ?
Dit cet animal plein de rage :
Tu seras châtié de ta témérité.

— Sire, répond l'agneau, que votre majesté
Ne se mette pas en colère ;
Mais plutôt qu'elle considère
Que je me vas désaltérant
Dans le courant,

Plus de vingt pas au-dessous d'elle ;
Et que par conséquent, en aucune façon,
Je ne puis troubler sa boisson.

— Tu la troubles ! reprit cette bête cruelle ;
Et je sais que de moi tu médis l'an passé.
— Comment l'aurais-je fait si je n'étais pas né ?
Reprit l'agneau ; je tette encor ma mère.

— Si ce n'est toi, c'est donc ton frère.
— Je n'en ai point.

— C'est donc quelqu'un des tiens ;
Car vous ne m'épargnez guère,
Vous, vos bergers, et vos chiens.
On me l'a dit : il faut que je me venge. »

Là-dessus, au fond des forêts
Le loup l'emporte, et puis le mange,
Sans autre forme de procès.

MAURICE BOUTET DE MONVEL / *"Le Loup et l'agneau"*

limp, no longer living form hanging from the raging wolf's mouth. One can scarcely fail to be moved by the terrible poignancy of Boutet de Monvel's interpretation. I think of these fine, softly colored, and economically conceived drawings as a musical accompaniment to the La Fontaine fable, harmonic inventions that color and give fresh meaning in much the same way that a Hugo Wolf setting illuminates a Goethe poem.

Relating such animated images to musical expression might appear too personal an identification for it to have any validity in the analysis of another artist's work. It is, of course, impossible to know whether Boutet de Monvel related his own work to music, but it is difficult for me not to think so. In the case of Randolph Caldecott, it is impossible to imagine his not being conscious, at least to some extent, of his musical sympathies. His pictures abound in musical imagery; his characters are forever dancing and singing and playing instruments. More to the point is his refinement of a graphic counterpart to the musical form of theme and variations, his delightful compounding of a simple visual theme into a fantastically various interplay of images.

Caldecott's pictures for *The Queen of Hearts* take off sedately enough; they state his theme (The Queen of Hearts, she made some tarts) simply and straightforwardly. Then begin the purely Caldecottian inventions, the variations that elaborate the nursery rhyme into an uproar of comical complications. He accomplishes this, not with flowing, sequential drawings across each page, but with tremendously animated scenes that rush from page to page. The crescendo peaks at the line "And beat the Knave full sore": in the background, Caldecott portrays the Knave being soundly beaten by the King to the

rhythm of a minuet danced gracefully in the foreground by a lady and gentleman of the court. Another
Caldecott book, *The Three Jovial Huntsmen*, is a
veritable song-and-dance fest with its syncopated
back-and-forthing between words and pictures. It has
a galloping rhythmic beat that is irresistible.

The sympathy I feel between the visual and the
musical accounts for my notion that I am setting a
text to pictures, much as a composer sets a poem to
music, and I have found that telling a story by means
of related, sequential pictures allows me to "compose"
with assurance and freedom. I do not, however, equate
the musical approach to sequential drawings. George
Cruikshank's pictures for the first English Grimm
definitely qualify as self-contained, full-page illustrations—the very opposite of the animated sequence and,
as far as I am concerned, the most difficult of forms to
bring alive. But there is nothing inanimate about the
Cruikshank pictures. They have a restlessness and
noisiness that are true qualities of childhood and the
lifeblood of the Grimm tales.

In our own day, André François is expert at
achieving liveliness within the full-page picture. His
vivid arrangements of shape and size on the page
make for an original and zany sense of animation.
His illustrations for John Symonds's *Tom and Tabby*
have a massive grandeur that yet contains an infinity
of lively detail.

Tomi Ungerer, in his illustrations for *Flat Stanley*
by Jeff Brown, cleverly avoids the inert full-page picture. He solves the problem through a sequence of
movement, not within each individual page, but from
page to page. Imaginative manipulation of space and
deft use of color give the happy effect of pictures
dancing through the book.

The little colored picture books William Blake intended for children are set apart by his incomparable genius. How beautifully his *Songs of Innocence* and *Songs of Experience* could be set to music, and how beautifully Blake did "set" them. The intensely personal images seem the very embodiment of his poetry. His inspired interweavings of ornament, illustration, and calligraphy animate the spirit of the poems and create a transcendent vision of otherworldliness. And it is all expressed with an economy only the masters achieved.

The musical analogy and its relevance to my own work is nowhere more apparent than in my illustrations for the picture books of Ruth Krauss. Her lovely and original poetry has a flexibility that allowed me the maximum space to execute my fantasy variations on a Kraussian theme, and to pursue my devotion to the matter of music.

[*1964*]

Mother Goose

Only Mother Goose, that doughty old wonder bird, could have survived the assiduous attention of generations of champions and detractors, illustrators and anthologists. More than merely survive, she has positively flourished—younger, fresher, and more vigorous than ever: witness the publication of Mother Goose books of every shape and size that has continued for generations, including the dozens now on the market in America. Among the most popular of this latter group is *The Real Mother Goose*, being issued this fall in a fiftieth-anniversary edition by Rand McNally and bearing on its cover a commemorative gold seal. The name and the seal raise a basic and puzzling question: Is there a *real* Mother Goose? The answer lies in an exploration of the origins of the Mother Goose rhymes and perhaps some assessment of the art that has illustrated them.

It is fairly well agreed that the earliest use of the name Mother Goose in the English language dates from a translation of the Perrault fairy tales, *Contes de ma mère l'Oye*, published in England in 1729. But the man who first took the name and gave it to a collection of traditional verses was John Newbery, who published his *Mother Goose's Melody* in 1765. After that, the name was retained only in America; the English usually refer to the works of Mother Goose simply as nursery rhymes, songs, jingles, or melodies. So any collection of Mother Goose rhymes confronting the bewildered purchaser is, strictly speaking, just as "real" as the Rand McNally edition, perhaps even more real, depending on the particular selection of rhymes and the perception of the illustrator.

Transmitted almost entirely by word of mouth, Mother Goose rhymes span an immense stretch of time, from the lovely "White Bird Featherless," which appears in Latin in the tenth century, up to "Horsey, Keep Your Tail Up," a popular commercial song of the 1920s. The origin of this potpourri of anonymous rhymes is described by Iona and Peter Opie, authors of the most authoritative collections of Mother Goose ever published, *The Oxford Nursery Rhyme Book* and the comprehensive *Oxford Dictionary of Nursery Rhymes*, from which I have borrowed much of my historical data. The *Dictionary*, a work of remarkable scholarship, is filled with a wealth of lore and generously sprinkled with some of the best examples of art illustrating Mother Goose.

The Opies note that the overwhelming majority of nursery rhymes were not originally composed for children and that many would be *verboten* to children in the original wording. (The only "true" nursery rhymes, those specifically composed *for* children, are the rhyming alphabets, the lullabies, and the infant amusements, or poems, accompanying a game created before 1800.) This genesis explains the earthy, ambiguous, double-entendre quality of so many of the verses—that lusty dimension too often missing in modern editions. The boring custom of passing over a witty, rambunctious, sometimes little-known verse ("I had a little husband, / No bigger than my thumb," for example), in favor of a pallid one such as "Mary Had a Little Lamb," adulterates the full flavor of Mother Goose and undermines the value of any given collection.

Even before John Newbery officially credited them to Mother Goose, the rhymes had their detractors. Negative criticism began as early as 1641 and has continued ever since. William and Ceil Baring-Gould, in the introductory chapter to their informative and lively *Annotated Mother Goose*, quote a Mr. Geoffrey Handley-Taylor of Manchester, England, who condemns at least a hundred of the rhymes for their unsavory elements. In 1952, he listed a series of—in his estimation—ghastlinesses that occur in the typical collection: one case of death by shriveling, one case of body snatching, one allusion to marriage as a form of death, nine allusions to poverty and want, and so inanely on. No comment from Mother Goose. That indefatigable lady has been too preoccupied in promulgating her poetry, busily adding to and enlarging her conglomerate collection with snatches of ballads, bits of political satire, snips of plays, folk songs, street cries, proverbs, and all manner of lampooneries.

The poets have repeatedly testified to the greatness of Mother Goose. Walter de la Mare wrote that many of the verses are "tiny masterpieces of verbal craftsmanship." Her rhymes "free the fancy, charm tongue and ear, delight the inward eye." Robert Graves claims the best of the older ones are nearer to poetry than the greater part of *The Oxford Book of English Verse*. G. K. Chesterton suggested that the line "Over the hills and far away" is one of the most beautiful in all English poetry.

The powerful rhythms of the verses combined with

their great strength and resonance account largely for their appeal to the child's inborn musical fancy. But there is more to the rhymes than music. Andrew Lang called them "smooth stones from the brook of time, worn round by constant friction of tongues long silent" —an image that suggests the presence of elusive, mythic, and mysterious elements transcending the nonsense.

This elusive quality of the verses—that something more than meets the eye—partially explains the unique difficulty of illustrating Mother Goose. For a start, they have about them a certain baldness that betrays the unwary artist into banalities. Another difficulty is related to that quality of the verses de la Mare described as "delighting the inward eye." Characteristic of the best imaginative writing, they evoke their own images, thus placing the artist in the embarrassing position of having to contend with Mother Goose the illustrator as well as the poet.

To make things more difficult, there is no room here for a mere show of sensibility, as some artists might get away with, for example, when illustrating the poetry of Robert Louis Stevenson or even the fairy tales of Andersen and Grimm. If full measure of the rhymes isn't taken in the pictures, then the artist has failed Mother Goose. And her revenge is swift, for no other writing I know of so ruthlessly exposes the illustrator's strengths and inadequacies.

So it is with trepidation that the artist must confront this formidable muse. There are basically two approaches. First, the direct, no-nonsense approach that puts the facts of the case into easy, down-to-earth images: Miss Muffet, her tuffet, curds, whey, and spider, all clearly delineated. This kind of illustrating does not pretend to any profound leaps of the imagination or depths of interpretation. It respectfully translates the literal truth into literal images. It is honest, attractive, and, I imagine, for the literal-minded child, the best possible accompaniment to the rhymes.

Blanche Fisher Wright's illustrations for *The Real Mother Goose* accomplish all this and a bit more. Despite a somewhat humorless touch, they have great charm and vigor; best of all, they manage to achieve that air of coziness and warmth so essential to the baby book. The sentimentalized Art Nouveau style (the pictures date from 1916) helps to enhance the snug effect by ringing the pictures round the verses and locking them safely in. If these illustrations do not catch the spirited quality of the verses or perform in an imaginative counterpoint to them, if they obstinately face away from the dark side of the matter and maintain a too-sunny disposition, they still have the virtue of honest homeliness.

For a more perceptive interpretation of Mother Goose, one must look elsewhere. Not, I hope, at *The Little Mother Goose*. Jessie Willcox Smith's illustrations, which were done around 1912, are hopelessly alien to the spirit of the rhymes. Pudgy, prissy pictures, some in clotted colors that dissolve in soggy sentiment, make for a volume that sweetens rather than interprets the verses.

In the 1870s, Walter Crane and the great English color printer Edmund Evans (whose pioneer work also made possible many of the Caldecott and Greenaway books) collaborated on *The Baby's Opera*, an illustrated edition of nursery rhymes set to traditional music. Crane was a tireless and adroit designer. In his hands a child's picture book became a matter of art. Everything is neatly balanced in *The Baby's Opera*, from the busybody activities of the tiny drawings decoratively arranged around the music to the cleverly spaced full-page pictures. There are devilish bits of action going on in corners, and an abundance of detail and subtle color throughout. But there is a flaw in this little book and it lies, ironically enough, deep within its superstructure of design. It is a breath too designed, thus fatally imprisoning the life within its pages.

Early in 1878, Randolph Caldecott began his illustrations for some of the better-known nursery rhymes, and no artist since has matched his accomplishments. Caldecott breathed life into the picture book. The design of his books, so seemingly casual, allowed him the greatest possible freedom in interpreting the verses. I spoke earlier of two basic approaches to illustrating the rhymes, the first being the more literal, direct approach; the second is the way Caldecott chose. As in a song, where every shade and nuance of the poem is heightened and given greater meaning by the music, so Caldecott's pictures illuminate the rhymes. This is the *real* Mother Goose—marvelously imagined improvisations that playfully and rhythmically bounce off and around the verses without ever incongruously straying. If any name deserves to be permanently joined with that of Mother Goose, it is Randolph Caldecott. His picture books should be among the first volumes given to every child.

Kate Greenaway, born the same month and year as Caldecott, was yet another contender for the honor of illustrating Mother Goose. Though probably more popular than Caldecott in her own time and certainly in our own, she can't hold a candle to him. When Caldecott's *Hey Diddle Diddle* was about to be published, Miss Greenaway had an opportunity to see some of the originals, and in a letter to a friend she wrote: "They are so uncommonly clever. The dish running away with the spoon—you can't think how

much he has made of it. I wish I had such a mind."
Alas, she didn't and knew it. Her *Mother Goose or The
Old Nursery Rhymes* is, after Caldecott, an awful let-
down. It is the great ancestor of the sentimental
Mother Goose books, and it is hard not to blame Kate
Greenaway for founding the line. For all its delicacy
of design and exquisite color, for all its refinement of
taste, there is little of the real Mother Goose in this
lovely but antiseptic affair. The rhymes have been
flounced out in a wardrobe of quaint Greenaway
frocks, and they look stiff and inanimate; Greenaway's
surface charm does not mitigate the atmosphere of
chilly Victorianism at the heart of her prim interpretation. See, for example, the two disdainful young
ladies who seem to rush off in shocked distaste at
the amusing verse they supposedly illustrate. All they
lack are scented hankies to disguise the bad odor of
Goosey Goosey Gander.

If Greenaway fails, perhaps it is due most of all to
her error in tangling with Mother Goose, a doomed
relationship that glaringly exposed her shortcomings.
When Greenaway illustrates Greenaway, as in her
tiny, sparkling almanacks, she ranks with the best.

A spiritual descendant of Caldecott is L. Leslie
Brooke (1862–1940), who illustrated, besides his more
famous Johnny Crow books, a number of Mother
Goose collections. The best of the lot is *Ring O' Roses*.
Brooke's unabashed admiration for Caldecott is reflected in every aspect of this book, from the clever
juxtaposition of black-and-white drawings and color
pictures to his manner of animating the verses with a
sequence of pictures that both amplify and deepen
them. The Brooke illustrations convey a tremendous
robustness and are very funny in the real old Mother
Goose way. And *Ring O' Roses* is no mere pastiche

Caldecott. The pictures are pure Leslie Brooke in flavor, the toasty warm, ample flavor that can only be English.

The Mother Goose book I like best, after Caldecott, is *The Only True Mother Goose Melodies*, a reproduction (published by Lothrop, Lee and Shepard in 1905) of an edition published in Boston in 1833 by Munroe and Francis, which in turn was possibly a pirated edition of the John Newbery *Mother Goose's Melody* of 1765. The anonymous pictures, though badly reproduced, are the very essence of Mother Goose— intensely alive, exceedingly droll ("To bed to bed says sleepy head," depicts a perfect moron type dropping turtles into a cooking pot). I agree with the Reverend Edward Everett Hale, who wrote in the introduction to this book that the artist who depicted the man in the moon (possibly Abel Bowen) ranks among "the original artists of the world." This picture graphically conceptualizes two aspects of nursery rhymes that, together, reveal a partial portrait of Mother Goose. A brick wall divides the picture through the center; on the right we see, vigorously drawn, a typical, earthy Mother Goose buffoon slopping cold plum porridge over his head, while to the left—gracefully poised in midair, with one arm arched over the crescent moon and half his figure in mist—floats the ambiguous man in the moon, secret and poetic. This is my favorite Mother Goose illustration.

What does Mother Goose have to say about her illustrators? Happily, nothing. But in the introduction to the 1833 edition of *The Only True Mother Goose Melodies*, she does have a bit to say about herself:

Fudge! I tell you that all their [critics of her rhymes] batterings can't deface my beauties, nor their wise pratings

The man in the moon came down too soon
    To inquire the way to Norridge;
The man in the south, he burnt his mouth
    With eating cold plum porridge.

ANONYMOUS / *The Only True Mother Goose Melodies*

equal my wiser prattlings; and all imitators of my refreshing songs might as well write a new Billy Shakespeare as
another Mother Goose—we two great poets were born
together, and we shall go out of the world together.
      No, no, my Melodies will never die,
      While nurses sing, or babies cry.

Modesty never did become her.

                                                    [*1965*]

Randolph Caldecott

Caldecott's work heralds the beginning of the modern picture book. He devised an ingenious juxtaposition of picture and word, a counterpoint that never happened before. Words are left out—but the picture says it. Pictures are left out—but the word says it. In short, it is the invention of the picture book.

Caldecott's *Hey Diddle Diddle* and *Baby Bunting* exemplify his rhythmic syncopation of words and images—a syncopation that is both delightful and highly musical. The characters leap across the page, loudly proclaiming their personal independence of the paper. In most versions of *Hey Diddle Diddle*, the cow literally jumps over the moon. But here the cow is merely jumping: the moon sits on the horizon in the background and, from our perspective, only gives the *appearance* of being under the cow. In this way, Caldecott is being exceedingly logical, since he obviously knows that cows can't jump over the moon. But within his logic he shows you, on the color page, two pigs dancing, the moon smiling, the hen and the rooster carrying on—all of it entirely acceptable to him and to us. Yet Caldecott won't go beyond a certain "logical" point: the cow *seems* to be jumping over the

So there was an end of one, two, and three,
Heigho, says ROWLEY!
The Rat, the Mouse, and the little Frog-gee!
With a rowley-powley, gammon and spinach,
Heigho, says ANTHONY ROWLEY!

RANDOLPH CALDECOTT / *(above) Baby Bunting (below) A Frog*
He Would A-wooing Go

moon, but in fact it's just leaping on the ground. Still, this is bizarre enough to make the milkmaid drop her pail of milk.

When you turn the page to read "The little Dog laughed to see such fun," you might well take this line as a reference to the cow jumping over the moon. It refers, however, to the spilt milk—or whatever was in that pail—now being gobbled up by the two pigs, while the cow stares from the corner, watching it all happen, and the maid looks down, perplexed, perhaps annoyed. So Caldecott has interjected a whole new story element solely by means of the illustrations, adding and compounding image upon image.

The situation in *Baby Bunting* is a bit more conventional: the baby is being dressed, Father's going a-hunting, looking a little ridiculous as he disappears behind a wall, followed by that wonderful dog trotting after him. But Father's frantic hunting is ineffectual, and all comes to naught. So they rush off to town to buy a rabbit skin. And this, of course, is Caldecott cutting up: the father dressed in hunting regalia with his dog, unable to kill a rabbit, finally winding up in town to *buy* the skin.

Father brings the rabbit skin home to wrap the Baby Bunting in, and what follows is a scene of jollity: the baby dressed in that silly garment, everyone rushing around, pictures on the walls from other Caldecott picture books. Then there is the lovely illustration of Mama and Baby.

And now Caldecott does the unexpected. The rhyme ends ("To wrap the Baby Bunting in"), but as you turn the page you see Baby and Mother strolling—Baby dressed in that idiotic costume with the ears poking out of her head—and up on the little hillside a group of rabbits playing. And the baby—I'd give anything to have the original drawing of that baby!

—Baby is staring with the most perplexed look at those rabbits, as though with the dawning knowledge that the lovely, cuddly, warm costume she's wrapped up in has *come* from those creatures. It's all in that baby's eye—just two lines, two mere dashes of the pen, but it's done so expertly that they absolutely express . . . well, anything you want to read into them. I read: astonishment, dismay at life. Is this where rabbit skins come from? Does something have to die to dress me?

After the comedy of what has preceded, this last scene is especially poignant. Caldecott is too careful and too elegant an artist to become melodramatic; he never forces an issue, he just touches it lightly. And you can't say it's a tragedy, but something hurts. Like a shadow quickly passing over. It is this which gives a Caldecott book—however frothy the verses and pictures—its unexpected depth.

Caldecott is an illustrator, he is a songwriter, he is a choreographer, he is a stage manager, he is a decorator, he is a theater person; he's superb, simply. He can take four lines of verse that have very little meaning in themselves and stretch them into a book that has tremendous meaning—not overloaded, no sentimentality anywhere. Everybody meets with a bad ending in *A Frog He Would A-wooing Go*. Frog gets eaten by a duck, which is very sad, and the story usually closes on that note. But, in Caldecott's version, he introduces, oddly enough, a human family. They observe the tragedy much as a Greek chorus might— one can almost hear their comments.

In the last picture, we see only Frog's hat on a rock at the stream's edge, all that remains of him. And standing on the bank are a mother, father, and two children. This is startling until you realize what Calde-cott has done. It's as though the children have been watching a theatrical performance, and they are terribly upset. There are no words—I'm just inventing what I think it all means: Frog is dead, it alarms them, and, for support, they are clinging to their parents. The older child, a girl, clutches her father's arm; the younger holds fast to his coat. The mother has a quiet, forlorn expression on her face. Very gently, she points with the tip of her parasol toward the stream and the hat. The father looks resigned. They're both conveying to the children, "Yes, it is unfortunate, but such things do happen—that is the way the story ended, it can't be helped. But you have us. Hold on, everything is all right." This is impressive in a picture book for children.

[*1978*]

Hans Christian Andersen

In a tumbledown cottage snugly thatched by nesting storks, with starlings twittering in the collapsed dovecote, and buckbean and yellow iris growing all around—that's the place to write about Hans Christian Andersen. Or, if one prefers the city, in an old, old house with pointed gables, beetling bay window, and a carved façade that has gargoyles leering from between tulips and twining hops—an ancient house filled with rickety furniture, faded portraits, and forgotten toys, all whispering, groaning, bemoaning the old days, the good days, the bright and shiny days when roses bloomed in vases and life teemed through the now-vacant rooms. The charm of either setting would be just right for thinking about Andersen. As it is, the unromantic city of New York in the year 1966, a decade short of the hundredth anniversary of Andersen's death, must do for me. And it does surprisingly well, granted that you stop your ears, turn off the telephone, and submerge yourself entirely in Andersen's poetry.

For a week I was oblivious of everything but the sound and imagery of Andersen. The tremendous hubbub of Andersen filled all the cracks of my brain like his favorite Danish wind that goes whistling, whoosh-ing, and galumphing through the cracks of dreaming old oak trees and over mysterious marshlands. I admit to going into that week ready to find out this teller of tales for a sentimental impostor who usurped the title "mythmaker of the nineteenth century." I returned from the week in awe of his accomplishments.

My seven-day sojourn in Andersen country was touched off by Monica Stirling's recently published biography of Andersen, *The Wild Swan*, which left me frustrated and annoyed with Miss Stirling and her subject. Why another biography unless it serves to illuminate the man and his work? But other than setting the events of his life in a historical context broader than that in most other biographies, Miss Stirling offers nothing significantly new. Here are the familiar quotes from letters and diaries (irritat-ingly few pertaining to his work) and the obligatory *tableaux vivants* of his life: early poverty, insecurity, humiliating dependence, dread of insanity, thwarted love, international success, famous visit with Dickens, homage from Odense, etc., all of which have been covered many times.

The best lines in *The Wild Swan* are those de-scribing Isak Dinesen and her devotion to Andersen's tales. Miss Stirling quotes her, when she was very old, demanding a book on her way to bed: "Where's my Andersen?" In her last years, Dinesen felt that she had lived more courageously than she would have had she not read Andersen throughout her life. Those few lines imply more of Andersen's power than anything else Miss Stirling tells us.

Andersen set the mode for his biographers with the opening line of his autobiography: "My life is a fairy tale." Unfortunately, biographers took him literally and perpetuated ad nauseam the stereotype of the poor cobbler's son who found fame and glory. It is sad that the important results of Danish scholarship on Andersen—criticism, essays, comprehensive editions of letters—have not been made available in English translation. Until they are, we must content ourselves with sentimental rehashings of his life. In Miss Stirling's words (couched in the tedious, child-imaged metaphors traditionally reserved for Andersen): "There are indeed fairy-tale elements in the story of the penniless cobbler's son who, after slaying many a dragon, won fame, fortune and the friendship of princes, but it is also a tragic story, in some ways the archetype of the artist's life-story." Yes, it is a wonderful story; but we've heard it all before. To name just a few versions: Jean Hersholt told it in his lengthy preface to *The Complete Andersen*; Signe Toksvig told it in what is considered one of the most authoritative biographies of Andersen; and Rumer Godden told it succinctly and I think best in her *Andersen: A Great Life in Brief.*

Besides supplying all the traditional anecdotes of the poet's life, Rumer Godden employs her delicate gifts of perception in a fascinating analysis of Andersen's work—it was this that set me to reading the fairy tales. One can quote endlessly from Miss Godden's book:

"For all their fantasy, [Andersen's tales] are life, universal, eternal; for all their lightness of touch, they are serious." "Andersen's own writing has economy and strength, an inexorableness that is sometimes so cruel that it is not for children at all; it is witty, ironical and humorous, and, though it can be intensely poignant and poetical, it is always crisp." "Each story has the essence of a poem, and a poem is not prose broken into short lines, but a distilling of thought and meaning into a distinct form, so disciplined and finely made, so knit in rhythm, that one word out of place, one word too much, jars the whole. In Andersen we are never jarred and it is this that gives the Tales their extraordinary swiftness." "His stories are parables and have meanings that sound on and on—sometimes over our heads—after their last word is read. He was a poet and knew the whole gamut of feeling from ecstasy to black melancholy and horror." Comments such as these penetrate the stereotyped portrait of the ungainly boy who grew up to write sentimental tales for children.

Andersen's eminence is indisputable, not as the poet who revolutionized the Danish language and wrote sublime parables, but simply as a successful writer of children's stories. Yet Andersen had no wish to write only for children. It was when he discovered that fairy tales allowed him surprising freedom to express his more intimate thoughts and feelings that he committed himself to them. By developing and varying this form, he ended by addressing the adults more often than the children.

"It is easy," Andersen said of his tales. "It is just as you would talk to a child. Anyone can tell them." This casual remark sums up the stylistic shock that confronted his first readers. By breaking with the stilted, formal literature of his day (and the very style that makes his autobiography and novels, in Miss Godden's words, "verbose and boring"), Andersen found himself.

"It's not writing, it's talking," said one irritated critic when the first tales were published. Another found them inspiring: "A new prose was born in Danish literature; the language acquired grace and color, the freshness of simplicity." It acquired a new diction full of familiar colloquialisms, whimsical transitions, short, explosive, everyday slang words, most of them, according to the Danes, untranslatable.

It is amazing that Andersen survived the early translations with any reputation at all. Alterations of plot, amputations of maxims and climaxes, descriptive sections arbitrarily lopped off, and, worst of all, the heavy, turgid, Victorian style in place of Andersen's racy prose—all were common offenses. Happily, such translations are a thing of the past. The only complete edition of the fairy tales in English (168 in all) is the one published by the Heritage Press in 1942 in the scrupulous though not inspired translation by Jean Hersholt. According to critics who know Danish, one of the more recent translators, R. P. Keigwin, catches the Andersen sound and color as never before in English.

When I began rereading the tales, my feelings, as I say, were ambivalent, in spite of the new picture of Andersen I had gleaned from Rumer Godden, the Danish writers Bo Gronbech and Erik Dal, and an interesting essay by Edmund Gosse, all committed admirers of Andersen. On the other side of the fence is P. L. Travers, and I found myself agreeing with her words in a recent article on fairy tales: "How much rather would I see wicked stepmothers boiled in oil—all over in half a second [referring to Grimm]— than bear the protracted agony of the little mermaid or the girl who wore the red shoes. There, if you like, is cruelty, sustained, deliberate, contrived. Hans Andersen lets no blood. But his tortures, disguised as piety, are subtle, often demoralizing." That's the Andersen I remembered before I turned back to his stories: a sentimental, pious, sadistic man whose work bore no comparison with the fierce, honest, and wildly imaginative tales of Grimm. Armed with the fairy tales, I set out to rediscover Andersen for myself; my project—to read all the tales in the Keigwin edition and supplement this by dipping into the Hersholt collection.

I began with the first four tales, published in 1835, when Andersen was thirty years old—"The Tinder-Box," "Little Claus and Big Claus," "The Princess and the Pea," and "Little Ida's Flowers," the first three borrowed from Danish folk tales, only the last entirely original. Having read a hundred of the stories, I think it is safe to say that the best and worst of Andersen is exemplified in these four stories. It is hard to imagine that there could be a better story than "The Tinder-Box" in the entire collection. Its opening lines tumble you headlong into Andersen country: "Left, right! Left, right! . . . Down the country road came a soldier marching. Left, right! Left, right! . . . He had his knapsack on his back and a sword at his side, for he had been at the war, and now he was on his way home. But then he met an old witch on the road. Oh! she was ugly—her lower lip hung right down on her chest. 'Good evening, soldier,' she said, 'what a nice sword you've got, and what a big knapsack! You're a proper soldier! Now I'll show you how to get as much money as you want!' " Bang! The short sentences with their sharp, marching rhythm fling you into the story before you know what hit you, and it's over before you've caught your breath.

Just as Andersen could sympathetically identify with the private lives of cooking pots, bottles, birds, and flowers, so could he completely assume the role of soldier (he *was* a frustrated actor-playwright). There is a rowdiness in the telling of "The Tinder-Box," a vulgar concern with money and a ruthlessness of action that are typical of the soldier of fortune who has seen the horrors of war and is complacent in the presence of death.

"The Tinder-Box" retains certain qualities of the French fabliau—the lightness of tone and a traditional flippancy concerning morals—whereas "Little Claus and Big Claus" is more a taproom tale, coarse, witty, erotic, and fraught with intrigue. It is hilarious, brutal, full of slapstick touches: "Now, although he was an excellent man, the farmer had the strange failing that he never could bear the sight of a parish clerk; if he ever set eyes on a clerk, he flew into an absolute rage." How cleverly Andersen turns this into a witty rationalization for the goings-on between clerk and farmer's wife: "And that was just why this clerk had called in to pass the time of day with the farmer's wife, when he knew that her husband was away from home."

"Little Ida's Flowers," the only completely original tale in the first group of four, is also the poorest. There is occasionally a disquieting passivity about Andersen that I associate with those tales mainly concerned with children. At his worst, he dreadfully sentimentalizes children; they rarely have the spunk, shrewdness, and character with which he endows his inanimate objects. Ida, however, is not the worst of Andersen's little girls; she is fairly lively and the story has lovely touches that foretell the future poet. The problem is that realistic little Ida does not jibe with Andersen's whimsical flower fancies. With time he acquired greater finesse, but in my opinion only a few of the original stories (such as "The Steadfast Tin Soldier," "The Old House," "The Marsh King's Daughter," "Thumbelina," "The Emperor's New Clothes") match the perfection of his retellings, or reimaginings, of the old Danish folk tales.

It is a pity he sacrificed all of Ida's toughness in exchange for such sentimental and irritating creatures as the little mermaid, Karen in "The Red Shoes," and the little match girl, the heroines of his most famous original stories. "The Little Mermaid" ranked high in Andersen's own estimation and in that of his contemporaries; it is still, puzzlingly enough, one of the most popular of his tales. It is much less striking in theme and language than some of the earlier ones and has little of Andersen's special humor. Slow and ponderous, rooted in Andersen's earlier style (adapted, probably, from his adult mermaid play, *Agnete and the Merman*), it harks back to the conventional literature of his time.

Jean Hersholt nicely sums up "The Little Match Girl" in his preface to the complete fairy tales: "In the vice of occasionally stumbling across the trip cord of sentiment, face down into sentimentality, they [Dickens and Andersen] were literary twins. Dickens could have written 'The Little Match Girl' with his hands tied. Andersen could have created Little Nell without half trying." I differ with Hersholt only in that Dickens could never have managed to make his "Match Girl" as mercifully brief and to the point as Andersen did.

"The Red Shoes" is the worst of the lot. The arbitrary torments Andersen inflicts on Karen are sadistic and distasteful in the extreme and the tale's Christian sentiment rings false; here P. L. Travers is absolutely right.

But in the immense Andersen landscape, these few tales are merely flyspecks on the horizon. I recently read Herman Melville's essay on Hawthorne and found myself substituting "Andersen" for "Hawthorne" in one particular paragraph: "But it is the least part of genius that attracts admiration. Where

[Andersen] is known, he seems to be deemed a pleasant writer, with a pleasant style,—a sequestered,
harmless man, from whom any deep and weighty
thing would hardly be anticipated:—a man who
means no meanings. But there is no man, in whom
humor and love, like mountain peaks, soar to such a
rapt height, as to receive the irradiations of the upper
skies;—there is no man in whom humor and love are
developed in that high form called genius; no such
man can exist without also possessing, as the indis-
pensable complement of these, a great, deep intellect,
which drops down into the universe like a plummet."

It is sad that Andersen is admired only for "the least
part of his genius." He is infinitely more than a teller
of sentimental tales; he is a poet. Through the medium
of the fairy tale, he found his original voice, and once
he accepted the fact that this, not the novel or the play,
was the form that best suited him, he proceeded to
master his art.

Andersen was that rare anomaly, wise man and innocent child; he shared with children an uncanny
poetic power, the power of breathing life into mere
dust. It is the intense life—honest, ingratiating—
in Andersen's tales that makes them unique. Dis-
carded bits of bottle, sticks, doorknobs, and fading
flowers give voice to their love, anguish, vanity, and
bitterness. They reflect on their past joys, lost oppor-
tunities, and soberly ponder the mystery of death.
We listen patiently, sympathetically, to their tiny
querulous voices and the miracle is that we believe,
as Andersen did, as all children do, that the bit of
bottle, the stick, the doorknob are, for one moment,
passionately living. The best tales of Andersen have
this mixture of worldliness and naïveté that makes
them so moving, so honest, so beautiful.

Andersen's autobiography is to be found scattered

throughout the fairy tales. How poignant is his love for Jenny Lind as expressed in stories like "The Nightingale," "The Angel," and "The Snow Queen," how ridiculous in "The Top and the Ball" (here is the humor and irony lacking in all the biographical accounts of this episode in his life). He reveals his almost pathological sensitivity in "The Princess and the Pea"; his black pessimism in "A Good Temper," "The Shadow," "The Drop of Water"; self-derision in "The Shirt Collar," "The Fir Tree"; cynicism in "The Shepherdess and the Chimney Sweep," "The Darning Needle"; high spirits in "The Traveling Companion" and "The Emperor's New Clothes."

One of my favorite Andersen tales is "The Butterfly," written in 1860. In it he cruelly mocks his bachelorhood. The butterfly dallies too long making up his mind which flower to propose to. He finds the anemones "a trifle bitter in their outlook"; the violets too romantic; the tulips too showy; the daffodils too suburban, etc. "Like all young men, he had an eye for older girls." Spring and summer pass and youth has flown; the butterfly is desperate. He proposes to the mint. "Friendship, but nothing more!" she says. "I am old, and you are old. I dare say we might live for one another, but marry—no! Don't let's make fools of ourselves at our time of life." So the butterfly remains a bachelor. Winter approaches and he seeks shelter in a house with a cheery fire.

Here's how Andersen ends his tale: "Then he flew against the window-pane, where he was seen, admired and stuck on a pin in a box of curios. Could more have been done for him? 'Well, here I am on a stalk just like the flowers,' said the butterfly. 'I can't say it's altogether comfortable. I expect it's like being married: you're certainly pinned down then!' And the thought consoled him. 'Rather a poor consolation,' said the pot-plants in the parlour. 'Still, pot-plants aren't always to be trusted,' thought the butterfly. 'They have too much to do with human beings.' "

[*1966*]

Adalbert Stifter

Of the six tales Adalbert Stifter wrote for his book called *Colored Stones (Bunte Steine)*, only *Rock Crystal* has been translated into English; the fact that the Pantheon edition is back in print after ten long years is reason for rejoicing. Anyone fortunate enough to own a copy of the first edition, published in 1945, might feel that tampering with any detail of that lovely book—its splendid translation by Elizabeth Mayer and Marianne Moore, its faultless pictures by Josef Scharl—is an act of sacrilege. But those responsible for the "tampering" in this revised edition deserve only praise. The already admirable translation has had the benefit of a scrupulous polishing, a refinement of phrase and detail that Stifter, often regarded in German-speaking countries as the greatest prose writer of the nineteenth century, would have fully appreciated. A few of Josef Scharl's pictures—majestically simple pictures which, by virtue of their utter lack of sentimentality, reach deeply into the poignancy and drama of the story—have been judiciously shifted, thus putting to rights some minor confusions in the earlier edition. I found only one small defect retained from the original edition: the last sentence of the publisher's note almost apologizes for Stifter's seeming verbosity. Why encourage "the impatient reader [who] may do his own skipping"? Let him read elsewhere.

Recounting the plot of *Rock Crystal* is like reading an opera libretto without hearing the music. Briefly, the situation is this: Two children, Conrad and his little sister, Sanna, are overtaken by a snowstorm while on their way home from visiting their grandparents, who live in a neighboring valley. Although the road is familiar, they lose their way in the blinding snow and must spend the night in an ice cave on a glacier, up high on the mountain of Gars. They bravely fight off the sleep that could mean death by sipping black coffee extract their grandmother gave them to carry back to their parents, and in the morning they are found and brought safely home. The dramatic action occurs on the Holy Eve, or Christmas Eve; through the long, cold, silent night the children witness what no one in the valley can see—the awesome display of the heavens, the flashing of cosmic lights, the mystic night fading to morning. And Sanna, endowed with the clear, innocent vision of childhood, believes she has seen the Christ Child.

When first published in 1843, *Rock Crystal* was titled *Holy Eve*. Stifter later rewrote it and incorporated it in *Colored Stones*; as each of the stories *(Granit, Kalkstein, Turmalin, Katzensilber, Bergmilch)* was named after some mineral or semi-precious stone which symbolically characterizes it, *Holy Eve* became *Rock Crystal (Bergkristall)*, a title that evokes the intense beauty and rare distinction of this tale.

Colored Stones is Stifter's celebration of country people whose faith in God and reverence for nature commit them to the great unchanging values from which their lives derive harmony. In the political upheavals of 1848, Stifter saw these values threatened, and to some extent *Colored Stones* was written as a protest against the uncertainties of the time. In his introduction he refers to the prevailing criticism of his work: that it tiresomely depicts the minute, that it is overconcerned with ordinary, humble folk. The younger critics, particularly, felt Stifter was out of touch with his time. They failed to perceive that his stories are not time-bound and that, unlike the other Romantic writers (with whom he shared an intense love of nature), he based his work on firm moral convictions.

Stifter detested sensationalism and violence, and criticized his contemporaries for their inability to distinguish the significant from the insignificant. For him the seemingly small things of life were the most valuable, and poetry was to be found not in the epic and spectacular but in the unostentatious, self-sacrificing lives of inarticulate, hardworking country people.

More than anything else, Stifter was concerned for the children and the effects of revolution on their lives. In his own words, the job was "little by little to wipe out and make harmless the bad impressions which have come out of the evils of the time." All six tales in *Colored Stones* are about children; though they were not written specifically for children, Stifter was soon besieged by people asking permission to include passages in children's anthologies, and younger readers have always loved the tales.

Whatever the merits of the other five stories, *Rock Crystal* is unquestionably a masterpiece. The tale begins softly with a tribute to the wonder and solemnity of Christmas, contrasting the holy ceremonials of the church with simple domestic traditions. Then, in a sweeping flow of shapely sentences that allow the

eye to follow every measured movement, Stifter
evocatively describes the Bohemian landscape—nature
painting that is no mere backdrop but rather the
palpable essence of the story.

Rock Crystal is brilliantly designed to lead up to
and away from its central action, the children lost in
the snow. Stifter's controlled and lucid prose has so
completely familiarized the reader with the physical
setting that when the snow begins to fall we no longer
read so much as see and hear the great descending
silence. It is a terrifying sequence, and no matter how
often I read it, the suspense is terrible. Stifter renders
the children so convincingly and views the scene with
such quiet objectivity that, for all our certainty of a
happy outcome, concern for the children's survival is
overwhelming.

Conrad and Sanna are at first delighted with the
silent falling snow and set their feet playfully in the
thick patches. Then: "A great calm had descended . . .
and the whole forest was as though dead." The children, as silently, shrink into their coats and push on
through the deepening snow. With nothing explicit
said, we know that Conrad has slowly become aware
of the danger. His first concern is for his sister; he
bundles her up in his fur coat and puts his cap on her
head. He points out bits of still visible landscape to
keep up her courage, and she, with her unbounded
faith in Conrad's judgment and strength, has but one
answer to everything he says: "Yes, Conrad." The
entire episode is poignantly dotted with Sanna's gentle
"Yes, Conrad."

The suspense mounts with the boy's determination
to keep himself and his sister alive through the long
night in the ice cave and is ultimately dispelled with
the great shudder of light that arcs across the sky; it
is the dawn of Christmas morning and the mystery of

this holy day fuses with the children's triumph over death. Their rescue is briefly described. Conrad imagines he sees a dancing red flame in the snow. It is the rescue flag being waved. The children hear, "across the still blue distance, something like the long-sustained note of an alpenhorn." They are safe, and Stifter ends his tale by blending into its final pages perhaps his most significant theme, brotherhood. The village of Gschaid and the town of Millsdorf, long divided by mountains and customs, have forgotten their differences in the mutual effort to find the children. All is resolved, and Stifter's hymn of Christian faith and salvation, of a better life on earth based on the eternal values, comes to an end.

[*1965*]

George MacDonald

George MacDonald was a novelist, poet. mythmaker, allegorist, critic, essayist, and, in everything, a preacher. One of the towering and mystifying figures of Victorian literature, he wrote well over fifty books, of which only two, *At the Back of the North Wind* and *The Princess and the Goblin*, are still widely read. His main forte was fantasy—his remarkable power, in the words of W. H. Auden, to "project his inner life into images, events, beings, landscapes which are valid for all." For admirers of MacDonald, such as myself, his work has something of the effect of an hallucinatory drug. Finishing one of his stories is often like waking from a dream—one's own dream. The best of them stimulate long-forgotten images and feelings—the "something profound" that borders frustratingly close to memory without quite ever reaching it.

His fairy tale *The Lost Princess* (also known as *A Double Story* and *The Wise Woman*) has itself been lost. Soon after his death in 1905, it mysteriously disappeared from his publishers' lists on both sides of the Atlantic and has remained unavailable until now. The production and illustration of this new edition (published by Dent and Dutton) leave much to be desired, but since the "meaning, the suggestion, the radiance," as C. S. Lewis puts it, is "incarnate in the whole story," the text more than makes up for the format and the illustrations.

The Lost Princess strikes a very different note from MacDonald's earlier fairy tales. There is a falling off, not of creative power, but rather of his faith in moral power. This is a harsh, angry tale whose magic, unlike the crystal-clear fantasy of MacDonald's earlier stories, is black, erratic, and appears finally to be nearly impotent against the forces of evil.

The Lost Princess concerns two fearsome children, Princess Rosamond and Agnes, a shepherd girl. Both are badly corrupted by the illusion that they are *Somebody*. Rosamond is vicious, greedy, and prone to maniacal rages. "At last, when she had nearly killed her nurse, and had all but succeeded in hanging herself, and was miserable from morning to night, her parents thought it time to do something." Agnes, a poor child, has been ruined by her parents' overweening admiration. Her face "looked so simpering and mawkish and self-conscious and silly that it made the wise woman feel rather sick." It is difficult to decide which set of parents or which child is more dreadful: "What is there to choose between a face distorted to hideousness by anger, and one distorted to silliness by self-complacency?" MacDonald concludes: "On the whole, of two very unpleasant creatures, I would say that the king's daughter would have been the worse, had not the shepherd's been quite as bad."

Both girls are "treated," in a manner of speaking, by the wise woman, another incarnation of the mythic female—either a grandmother- or an earth-mother-type—who recurs in many of MacDonald's tales. The wise woman employs drastic means with

Rosamond. "For when people *will* be naughty they
have to be frightened, and they are not expected to
like it." After many painful trials, during which the
two girls magically exchange roles, Rosamond is faced
with the most terrible tests of all: she is put in the
wise woman's chamber of moods. In the first test,
Rosamond finds herself in her old nursery, where "her
little white rabbit came to meet her in a lumping
canter, as if his back were going to tumble over his
head." She fails this test because she loses her temper;
she fails the second one because, in her uncontrollable
rage, she unwittingly drowns a child—an episode that
has the terror of a nightmare. "Couldn't you help
me?" Rosamond finally asks piteously. "Perhaps I
could, now you ask me," answers the wise woman.
In the third test, she meets an enigmatic child and a
pretty winged horse; desperately struggling against
her own demon, Rosamond grows compassionate and
for the first time tastes the sweetness of humility. Her
regeneration has begun.

There is, however, no help for Agnes. The wise
woman puts her, "naked as she was born," into a
great hollow sphere where, after three lonely days, a
creature appears beside her. "All at once the creature
began to smile, but with such an odious self-satisfied
expression that Agnes felt ashamed of seeing her.
Then she began to pat her own cheeks, to stroke her
own body, and examine her finger-ends, nodding her
head with satisfaction." Agnes is perfectly aware that
the "ape-like creature" is only doing "outside of her
what she herself had been doing, as long as she could
remember, inside of her." But after her trial, Agnes
is as smug and obnoxious as ever. In the closing scene,
the wise woman wrathfully blames the two sets of
parents for the ruin of Rosamond and Agnes. She
punishes the king and queen by striking them blind,

while the shepherd and his wife are condemned to live with Agnes, who looks "white as death and mean as sin." There is some small hope at the end that these stubborn souls may yet be saved if they willingly turn to the wise woman for help.

The Lost Princess (1875) and *The Princess and Curdie* (1877) are the last major fairy tales MacDonald wrote for children, and in both of them the joyfulness of the early tales has been replaced by a grim, apocalyptic gloom. Evil partially triumphs in *The Lost Princess* and at the end of *The Princess and Curdie* sweeps everything before it. The two heroines of *The Lost Princess* are the very opposite of the lovely Princess Irene of *The Princess and the Goblin*. Unlike Rosamond and Agnes, Irene believes completely in her great-great-grandmother, who lives at the top of the staircase; she puts herself unquestioningly in her care and follows wherever her magic thread leads. Those who admire MacDonald for Irene and for Diamond, the gentle boy of *At the Back of the North Wind*, might very well be put off by the harshness of *The Lost Princess*. That would be a pity, for despite the sharp change of mood from the earlier fairy tales, *The Lost Princess* abounds in MacDonald's personal imagery and concerns. There are the familiar unearthly landscapes, the subtlety and seriousness with which he analyzes his characters' thoughts and feelings.

Best of all, there is MacDonald's extraordinary evocation of the dream. Beyond providing the personal motif of his work, dreams offered MacDonald freedom to examine his emotions behind a screen sufficiently remote and fantastic to safeguard his mid-Victorian audience from shock. Even more important, he shared the views of the early German Romantic writers, particularly Novalis and E. T. A. Hoffmann, whom he most admired. These pre-Freudian artists rebelled against the prevalent attitude that dreams were merely the meaningless rumblings of the brain. They equated dreams with emotional truth and imagination, and Novalis contended that life would have meaning only when it attained the spiritual, poetic truth of the dream. Rosamond, the lost princess, only begins to find herself in the mood—or dream—chambers of the wise woman.

MacDonald might have ended *The Lost Princess* with one of his favorite quotations from Novalis, a quotation he used as an epigraph for his first great fairy tale for adults, *Phantastes*, and which makes up the closing words of his last book, the dream romance *Lilith*: "Our life is no dream, but it should and will perhaps become one."

[*1966*]

Lothar Meggendorfer

In the winter of 1960, an old friend and fervent collector introduced me to the work of Lothar Meggendorfer. A book with the inviting title *Merry Company: A Funny Moveable Toy Book* was put into my hands. This same friend had already introduced me to earlier transformation books. He knew of my delight in animating figures on a page—of my wish to revive a popular device of the 1930s, the pop-up books of my childhood. With his collection at my disposal, I soon made acquaintance with some rare, fragile transformation books and mechanical toy books that went back to the seventeenth century, notably the flap books called harlequinades, which contain half-page overlays that transform one picture into another. All of these charming "trifles" were novelties for grownups. They had not yet been relegated to the nursery. It is strange and touching to think of a time when games and movable picture books were the domain of adults.

It was not until the mid-nineteenth century that such novelties were conceived exclusively as children's books. The artificial world of juvenile publishing had begun. There was Dean & Co., in London, specializing in mechanical books for children—and admirable ones they were, too. If there was a fault, it lay, perhaps, in Dean's presupposing what was good for children, the result being a rather bland image of a child's world that mirrored the Victorian ideal of childhood. Despite this, the quality of Dean's early work is vastly superior to the dull, pap-ish books children had to suffer through for generations after, including our own. In fact, the first pop-up published by Dean was far from dull or pap-ish. Issued about 1855, it was a lively, fresh version of *Little Red Riding Hood*. The primitive mechanics seem only to enhance this lovely book. It was followed a year later by a movable *Old Mother Hubbard*, a somewhat more intricate work containing mechanical figures activated by paper tabs at the bottom of each page. By the early sixties, Dean had published a number of "dissolving views" books and later improved the old flap pictures by issuing several transformation "pantomimes." While the methods employed might be different, the results were the same: the picture moved. A toy book, a fantastical book; in short, a dream come true. I discovered to my amazement that my pop-ups of the 1930s were the end and not the beginning of a form. And delightful as those books are, they appeared to me now as a dropping off, a regression to the crude beginnings of that form.

But between Dean and my pop-ups there was Lothar Meggendorfer, who used the mechanical toy book to exercise his genius. This particular form allowed him to indulge to the full, but with amazing control, his inspired fancies. By the 1890s, he had turned the mechanical toy book into a work of art. He was the supreme master of animation; every gesture, both animal and human, coarse and refined, was conveyed via the limited but, in his hands, versatile technique of movable paper parts. But let me return to that winter of 1960 when I saw my first Meggendorfer.

Again, the alluring title *Merry Company: A Funny Moveable Toy Book*, a difficult title for any artist to live up to. (The original German title is *Lustiges Automatentheater*.) This book is full of glorious Meggendorfers, chief among them the effete Dancing Master. He is poised delicately on one toe, violin tucked under chin, and is arrayed in breeches, pointed shoes, and powdered wig. He stands on a polished floor against an eighteenth-century background very Mozartian in flavor. His face is coarse—until you pull the paper tab and instantly our musician is transformed. His eyes roll swooningly upward, lifting the dark, arched eyebrows. He is transfigured by the sound of his music. The delicate, smooth gestures of the wrist, elbow, and toe turn him into an utterly graceful and charming creature. He is meant to be comic and he is—but being a Meggendorfer, he is much more. The artist intended more than a passing joke on the cliché dancing master. And this is the key to Meggendorfer: His pictures don't merely move; they spring to life. Our little Dancing Master, by the power of music, is transformed into a gallant swain. Perfectly still, he is ridiculous. But when he moves, he is the embodiment of musical grace.

In a Meggendorfer archive I discovered the original drawing and assembled parts of my Dancing Master. It was with tremendous excitement that I examined my favorite picture rendered by Meggendorfer himself. I had always wondered what the original looked like and how much had been lost in the printing. The two versions are very different, but, in my opinion, Meggendorfer designed his pictures with the printed version in mind, and it seems to me that nothing at all is lost. The actual drawing is spontaneously rendered in watercolor. The figure and the background are sketchily outlined in ink and pencil and the color is casually washed in. The total effect is charming and luminous. Meggendorfer was a dashing draftsman. But the printed Dancing Master is quite different. The subtlety is all gone; the color is flattened and the outlines are rigid. Very little of the sketchiness (except for the dance floor) remains. The effect is greater vividness, and this, I am convinced, is what the artist intended. All the sweetness of rendering in the original is put into significant gesture. Meggendorfer would not have wanted us distracted by the *surface* of the picture—he is too good a performer for that. The original, so to speak, gives away the surprise. It is all there in the watercolor portrait of the Dancing Master. We see Meggendorfer's vision of the man and what he intends to do with him; the depth of the musician is made visible. In the printed version we see the quality of the man only when we pull the tab. And this is as it should be. What seems flat and funny is, suddenly, delightful and touching. It takes our breath away. The mechanical toy book had never done this before.

In older examples of the mechanical book, the action was sufficient—and varied enough from page to page to sustain interest. In Meggendorfer, there is no trifling movement. The gestures are precise and totally convincing for each individual creature. A horse does not move like a goat.

There is a cat in *Automatentheater*—a fierce, worried-looking cat. It sits on the edge of the tailor's ironing board, nervously eyeing the hot iron in the man's hand as it slowly approaches. We know from the verse that the overzealous tailor had at least once accidentally burned her tail. The cat's body is tense, the neck anxiously arched. When we pull the tab, the

LOTHAR MEGGENDORFER / *The original drawing of the Dancing Master*

tailor moves his iron carefully over a coat and approaches the tail, which is gradually withdrawn. The tailor seems very aware of the danger; his eyes grow larger as he gets close to the tail. In fact, they both know exactly what they are doing. The cat gives the show away by letting her tail reappear—just the tip of it, as though to prolong the game. It is an intimate, cozy picture. The particular character of Cat is neatly conveyed. The curious creature knows full well what might happen but clearly relishes the suspenseful play. The offended tail slips away just in time. It is a teasing game that only a cat could enjoy. And how swiftly the relationship between cat and tailor is established by just pulling down on a tab!

Lustiges Automatentheater is a masterpiece, and, to the dismay of collectors, it is only one of over one hundred books by Meggendorfer. In an article about the artist written by a Dr. Wilhelm Ruland for the newspaper *Beilage zur Allgemeinen Zeitung* in 1902, it is noted that more than a million copies of Meggendorfer books had been printed and sold by his publishers. Those publishers, Braun & Schneider in Munich and J. F. Schreiber in Esslingen, were, it is to be assumed, content. Meggendorfer was as well known, perhaps even better known, outside the world of toy books. He published, and contributed drawings to, the *Meggendorfer Blätter* as well as illustrating for the older and more famous *Fliegende Blätter*. And of all the superb *Münchener Bilderbogen*, his (with the possible exception of Wilhelm Busch's) are the finest.

Meggendorfer was that rare anomaly: an uncompromising artist who enjoyed a huge success. His intricate, elaborate, and very perishable books were best sellers. *Im Sommer* went through sixteen editions totaling thirty thousand copies, and *Im Winter*, eleven editions totaling twenty thousand copies (within just two years). *Internationaler Circus* ran through seven editions. How in the world could they ever manage to mass-produce such highly involved, elegant machinery? Slave labor, no doubt, or an altogether alien economy. Nevertheless, it is very gratifying to realize that Meggendorfer combined popular appeal with the highest aesthetic principles. He seems to say: It can be done.

One of the loveliest portraits in the Meggendorfer gallery is of the swans in *Nah und fern*. A woman and a young girl are standing by the side of a lake throwing food to the swans. The gentle movements of their arms and the graceful curvings of the great birds' necks have a measured, almost somnambulistic quality. One *could* speed up the action by pulling the tabs more quickly, but after some experience, one begins to sense the speed at which Meggendorfer must have intended these pictures to move. This scene insists on moving slowly. Its surreal enchantment is lost when one merely tugs at the tab. Meggendorfer assumed a certain degree of sensibility and imagination on the part of his readers.

"Der Papagei" is perhaps one of the most spectacular of all Meggendorfers. It is a tour de force of complex movement; but even here the artist does not lose sight of the essential action and he keeps faith with his bird. The parrot swings (on his stand) across the space of a double-page spread. The bird's body arches, its tail pulls back oarlike, and the bill snaps authoritatively and we *hear* that snap. There is even a flurry-of-feathers sound.

It is no surprise to find Meggendorfer obsessed with things musical. There seems to be a silent melodic accompaniment—a rhythmic line—to most of his animated scenes. Over and over again, he demonstrates his expert knowledge of the mechanics of musical instruments and synchronizes the gestures of his instrumentalists to an imaginary beat and tempo: cellist tapping time with his foot while he energetically bows his instrument. *Immer lustig* has a magnificent Kapellmeister—his face fixed in a frigid glare, arms stiffly outstretched and wrists expertly poised. Pull tab: arms deliberately move upward and then the lovely surprise: those wrists elegantly bend outward. There is a fat, jolly drummer beating a sharp tattoo (or slow, depending on your tab pulling or sense of rhythm). It is difficult to track down all the musicians, but I know of a maniacal pianist pounding his keyboard à la Liszt. His heaving shoulders and a white, painfully thick neck make him both amusing and very appealing. I am especially fond of a flutist called "Der musikalische Clown." He raises his puff-sleeved arms and with an eerily naturalistic, undulating movement adjusts instrument to mouth. It is extremely lifelike without sacrificing its otherworldly, Watteau-like atmosphere.

One must stop finally; there are too many worthy examples. It is an extraordinary fact that few *ordinary* Meggendorfer pictures exist. There are those, of course, that do merely move—the elephant, for example, raising his trunk in *Always Jolly*, the English edition of *Immer lustig*. But the well-known Great Lion (again from *Always Jolly*), who "merely" drops his massive jaw and swings his tail, is redeemed by a last-minute head-lowering that is terrifically threatening and a piece of mechanical workmanship only Meggendorfer would have bothered with.

I would like to conclude this Meggendorfer résumé with my two favorite books. One is a typical tab-pulling Meggendorfer and the other is a completely novel form of toy book. The former, *Reiseabenteuer des Malers Daumenlang und seines Dieners Damian,* is different only in that it is a continuous story. *Daumenlang* tells in words and moving pictures the adventures of a diligent painter and his rather hysterical manservant. Each page is another episode in their odd travels. In the picture captioned "Der Tiger kommt," Little Lord Thumb is busily plying his paintbrush, oblivious of all surroundings, while Damian, his head shaking in terror, points wildly at a tiger rolling its green eyes at them. This picture is a grand ballet of choreographed movements—an elegant counterpoint of all the characters animated at different tempos. The entire book is a virtuoso celebration of motion, as well as a carnival of animals in which Meggendorfer does full justice to the bear, snake, crocodile, ape, and other beasts.

Internationaler Circus is like no other Meggendorfer. In form, it is an elaborate pop-up book, or perhaps pop-out would best describe it. *Circus* is not actually a book at all but rather a series of panels hinged together, the whole thing working on the principle of a standing screen. The "book" fans out and each panel is a circus tableau. The backdrops are flat, representing spectators sitting in tiers. The crowd serves only as background, but Meggendorfer has gone to the trouble of characterizing everybody. Then there is a middle ground of action and a foreground. These are cardboard pull-outs attached to each panel. When they are fully extended, a tremendous sense of depth is achieved and we have a thrilling tumult, just what a circus should be: pretty girls leaping through hoops, horses prancing, monkeys performing tricks, and an orchestra blazing away. The color, excitement, and delirium of the circus are all there and the three-dimensional effect is breathtaking. I once arranged this book in a semicircle on the floor and seated a little boy in the middle of it all. He never spoke. He looked about him, slowly, and then at me, and I could sense his emotion. Meggendorfer never fails.

Present-day economy, alas, does not permit such grandiose flights of imagination. But the wish to animate is always there. It is the means by which the artist entices children into a book. Children are a discriminating and often reluctant audience; it is no mean feat, catching their attention. Meggendorfer enlarged the child's visual pleasure in a way that probably will never be duplicated. His work stands alone. What came after, the pretty pop-ups of my own childhood, was skimpy in comparison and, more to the point, was directed at a profitable, publishing-concocted child audience. Meggendorfer never condescended to children. He granted them, as he granted himself, a lively intellect and a cultivated visual taste. He knew that children observe life more cannily than adults, that they enjoy with a kind of sensual gusto the delights of color, shape, and movement. What he had to offer was the very best on the highest level. It is no accident that children delighted in his work, as did the adults who had the grace to remain children.

[*1975*]

Beatrix Potter / 1

For nearly fifty years Beatrix Potter lived with her parents and younger brother at No. 2 Bolton Gardens, Kensington. In her middle thirties she wrote *The Tale of Peter Rabbit* and for the first time— thanks to the encouragement of her publishers and friends, the Warne family—began to see a bit beyond her Kensington prison. This was the start of her creative life. She took an open stand against her family at the age of thirty-nine when she became engaged to Norman Warne, but his sudden death put an end to Miss Potter's hopes of escape from home. Finally, in 1913, at forty-seven, she managed to break the parental bond by marrying William Heelis; and thereafter the Beatrix Potter we know ceded place to Mrs. Heelis, loving wife, expert farmer, and breeder of Herdwick sheep. Her best work lay behind her, and gradually all trace of the artist vanished. When she died in 1943, her Sawrey neighbors mourned the loss of a hardworking farmer and an ardent protector of the English countryside (most of her money went to the National Trust to safeguard the beauties of the Lake District) rather than the famous author of the Peter Rabbit books.

Until now, what little knowledge we had of Beatrix Potter's life before the publication of *Peter Rabbit* we owed to her biographer, Margaret Lane. She has written: "If there were a mystery anywhere in this simplest and most innocent of lives, it would be in the silence and blankness stretched like a skin over the decade from her seventeenth to her twenty-seventh year." The publication of Beatrix Potter's journal of the years 1881 to 1897 puts an end to the mystery. The Potter admirer need not fear (or, even worse, be titillated by the prospect of) intruding upon dark secrets; Beatrix Potter tells us almost nothing we could not have surmised. The only "mystery" relating to the journal is the fact that it was written in code. Leslie Linder, in his introduction, describes the difficulties he encountered trying to break the code; one of the many problems was Miss Potter's nearly indecipherable handwriting and unorthodox spelling.

Beatrix Potter began her journal when she was fifteen and brought it abruptly to an end when she was thirty-one. It is not exclusively a diary or an autobiographical study. One finds frequent scraps of family gossip, social history, and politics, appreciations of paintings, descriptive sketches of human and animal friends. The journal is discursive, rambling, and most of the time makes mildly pleasant reading, but it is not nearly what we have come to expect from an artist's journal. Where is the intensive self-examination, the struggle of a creative spirit trying to find and assert itself? It is unfair, however, to dismiss Beatrix Potter, as revealed in her journal, as superficial. She did suffer, she did search, but in a manner befitting a very proper, well-bred, and therefore inhibited Victorian young lady, to whom any form of excess was distasteful. In her own words: "Artists certainly are a singularly nervous race."

If we put aside the romantic image of the artist, the journal becomes more interesting. The struggling young artist is there, but one must work hard to find her. And that suggests, perhaps, a second, more subtle code for the perceptive reader to break. Beatrix Potter led an intensely absorbed inner life, and she chose to express herself, as did most Victorian writers whether consciously or not, in a rather roundabout fashion. Loneliness was obviously the spur that drove her to keep a journal, but Miss Potter does not make much of that loneliness. There is no hint of self-pity or morbidity of mind, though she views herself harshly. At eighteen she writes: "I always thought I was born to be a discredit to my parents, but it was exhibited in a marked manner today. Since my hair is cut my hats won't stick on, and today being gusty, it must needs blow into the large fountain at the Exhibition, and drifted off to the consternation of my father, and the immense amusement of the spectators . . . If only I had not been with papa, he does not often take me out, and I doubt he will do it again for a time."

And, at twenty-nine, Miss Potter writes: "I am undeniably clumsy, but I think it is partly my back." Later that same year, there seemed no way out. "One must make out some way. It is something to have a little money to spend on books and to look forward to being independent, though forlorn." One pities her for assuming without question that she had such "defects of character" and wishes she could have observed and known people more in sympathy with her nature.

Whatever questionable effects parents, upbringing, and social restraints had on Beatrix Potter, she chose not to mourn over them in her private diaries. Her complaints took the form of frequent ladylike headaches (sometimes not so ladylike), and she seems to have let it go at that. In all the years of the journal, she records only one occasion when her "deplorable" father drove her to tears, though the few observations concerning her parents are caustic or ironic and leave no doubt as to how she felt toward them. "My father, always accustomed to get the newspapers on his mind, and in my opinion very unwell, was deplorable." Though deeply concerned during her mother's serious illness, she remains appallingly frank: "There is supposed to be some angelic sentiment in tending the sick, but personally I should not associate angels with castor oil and emptying slops."

I haven't any doubt that the journal was meant only for her own eyes; its tediousness is positive proof that she had no thought of posterity. (If we need further proof, the code should be enough.) However, in this case, tediousness becomes a virtue when we realize that, knowingly or not, she was practicing to become Beatrix Potter the artist. The minutiae she meticulously recorded from day to day are a direct clue to the character and strength of her art, since Miss Potter's best books grew out of this tight enmeshing of reality with a frank, honest, no-nonsense approach to fantasy. The journal of Beatrix Potter is an artist's journal. We are watching an artist learn her craft. Her purpose was to observe and record with the greatest possible accuracy the life around her. Through the tangle, one catches sight of a bright-eyed, tense young lady greedily hoarding bits of conversation and snips of information. In the privacy of her journal, this socially inhibited adolescent re-created the grownup chitchat, giving it form, mimicking and poking fun at certain individuals, laughing at their pomposities, and indulging in the kind of graceful and witty sociability that she felt excluded from in real life. Her journal is an enormous sketchbook in which she tried to teach herself how to see and write; it has a familiar Potter ring.

From the beginning, the journal displays her independent spirit. I particularly relish her attitude toward art school: "I may probably owe a good deal to Mrs. A. as my first teacher. I did to Miss Cameron, but I am convinced it lies chiefly with oneself." At eighteen she was already able to say, "I don't want lessons, I want practice. I hope it is not pride that makes me so stiff against teaching, but a bad or indifferent teacher is worse than none. It cannot be taught, nothing after perspective, anatomy and the mixing of paints with medium." She anxiously considers the worth of expensive art lessons: "Is the money being thrown away, will it even do me harm?" And she sums up the problem in her typically blunt, ironic manner: "It is tiresome, when you do get some lessons, to be taught in a way you dislike and to have to swallow your feelings out of considerations at home and there. Mrs. A. is very kind and attentive, hardly letting me do anything."

Her early visits to the art museums provoked a flood of criticism. Her taste is shaky and unorthodox, but considering the fact that she was first exposed to the masterpieces of the National Gallery in late adolescence and that she applied only her own homemade standards to works of art, she comes off surprisingly well. She gave them a hard Potter stare and nobody, not even Michelangelo, was spared. "No one will read this. I say fearlessly that the Michelangelo is hideous and badly drawn; I wouldn't give tuppence for it except as a curiosity." Turner comes off somewhat better. "Turner is the greatest landscape painter that ever has lived, far superior to Claude or the Dutch painters." She thinks a painting by Rubens "seems rather to want purpose and shadow, it was rather higgledy-piggledy." As for Rembrandt's four paintings at the Royal Academy of Arts Library, "Of the two small compositions of figures I could notice nothing particular, except that they were dark and Dutch. The two portraits were powerful in their way, but, if I had not known who they were by, I should not have looked at them with much interest." She added a footnote that gives her reason for not destroying the preceding remarks: "[They] are so amusing to me as representing childlike and simple, not to say, silly sentiments that have since passed away, that I preserve the greater part of them, though it is rather appalling to find one was such a goose only three years since." Gooselike, in some instances, they may be, but she underestimated her honest capacity to judge for herself and not be intimidated by undue reverence for the past.

The most fascinating passages in the journal are those relating to her own art and to the animals who later became the characters of her books. In one of the last entries, Beatrix Potter, now thirty, sketches a scene that evokes the spirit with which she was soon to embark on her life's work. "I think one of my pleasantest memories of Esthwaite is sitting on Oatmeal Crag on a Sunday afternoon, where there is a sort of table of rock with a dip, with the lane and fields and oak copse like in a trough below my feet, and all the little tiny fungus people singing and bobbing and dancing in the grass and under the leaves all down below, like the whistling that some people cannot hear of stray mice and bats, and I sitting up above and knowing something about them."

Her ability to hear "the whistling that some people cannot hear" and to know something about the stray mice and bats prefigures the microcosm Beatrix Potter so painstakingly, so brilliantly brought to life in her books. (When I recently read the books in chronological order, I became aware of a most curious phenom-enon. Her voice in *Peter Rabbit* seems to be on normal "ear level," but thereafter it becomes tiny, sharp as a needle, and, wonder of wonders, drops be-low ear level. Peter speaks from somewhere near your head, but the voices in *The Tailor of Gloucester* come from somewhere under the rug. By the time of *The Tale of Two Bad Mice*, the author has perfected her "miniature" voice; it is a kind of ventriloquist act that scales the voice down to mouse size. This could be dismissed as an aberration peculiar to me. Be that as it may, when I read *The Pie and the Patty-Pan*—my favorite Potter—her voice is dog-and-cat size.)

Beatrix Potter's many observations about animals and animal friends throughout the journal substantiate what one has always known from her books—that she was unmitigatingly honest about them, sometimes harsh, always adoring, but without any taint of senti-mentality. On a Sunday in October 1892, while photo-graphing in the woods, Beatrix happened on a rabbit caught in a snare and saved its life. "They are regular vermin, but one cannot stand by to see a thing mauled about from one's friendship for the race." She is care-ful not to show it to a favorite pet, the real Benjamin Bunny, but the smell of its fur on her dress "was quite enough to upset the ill-regulated passions of that ex-citable buck rabbit." She then proceeds to sum up Benjamin and all his race: "Rabbits are creatures of warm volatile temperament but shallow and absurdly transparent. It is this naturalness, one touch of nature, that I find so delightful in Mr. Benjamin Bunny, though I frankly admit his vulgarity. At one moment amiably sentimental to the verge of silliness, at the next, the upsetting of a jug or tea-cup which he im-mediately takes upon himself, will convert him into a demon, throwing himself on his back, scratching and spluttering. If I can lay hold of him without being bitten, within half a minute he is licking my hands as though nothing has happened. He is an abject coward, but believes in bluster, could stare our old dog out of countenance, chase a cat that has turned tail." She concludes with an anecdote. "Benjamin once fell into an Aquarium head first, and sat in the water which he could not get out of, pretending to eat a piece of string. Nothing like putting a face upon circumstances." How I wish she had illustrated that episode.

The journal or, as I prefer, sketchbook, is filled with other droll portraits like the one of Benjamin Bunny. Unfortunately, there are many more descriptions of visits in which the author tries painstakingly to set down every fragment of conversation, describe every turn of head and detail of costume. She captures too well the dullness of it all, but occasionally her little anecdotes have the surprising freshness and charm of a scene out of Jane Austen. Her portraits of town and landscape are, on the whole, overburdened with detail; but again, here and there, we stumble on flashes of her succinct and witty style. It develops before our eyes.

It is apparent throughout the sketchbook that Beatrix Potter was blessed with an impressive memory. She was aware of this, and many of the entries are obviously a kind of homework designed to exercise that precious faculty, to keep it sharp and quick. If some of these exercises make tedious reading, one can still appreciate their beneficial effects on Beatrix Potter. And sometimes the exercises are very evocative. "The pleasantest association of that pleasant room for me is of our teas there in the twilight. I hope I am not by nature greedy, but there was something rapturous to us London children in the unlimited supply of new milk. I remember always the first teas of the visit when we were thirsty and tired. How I watched at the window for the little farm-boy, staggering along the carriage-drive with the cans! It came up warm in a great snuff-coloured jug which seemed to have no bottom, and made the milk look blue. I seem to hear the chink of the crockery as the nurse-girl brought it out of the closet in the wall and laid the coarse, clean table cloth. I think the earthenware had a peculiar cool pleasant taste."

In her descriptive portraits, we can almost trace the origins of some of her famous characters. I cannot imagine a loyal Potterite who would not exclaim at this portrait of eighty-three-year-old Kitty Mac-Donald, the Potters' Scottish washerwoman: "She is a comical, round little old woman, as brown as a berry and wears a multitude of petticoats and a white mutch [linen cap]. Her memory goes back for seventy years and I really believe she is prepared to enumerate the articles of her first wash in the year '71." And: "Kitty was there helping, with quite a mountain of petticoats up the back of her. Standing beside Miss Duff, she reached about to her shoulders, a comical little object." Who else but the indefatigable, fastidious, comfortable, round, good-tempered hedgehog washerwoman, Mrs. Tiggy-Winkle herself! Though Beatrix Potter never referred to Kitty when she began *Mrs. Tiggy-Winkle* (some thirteen years after the above entries), an echo of her old delight in the Scottish washerwoman survives in a letter to Norman Warne describing the first drawings of her pet hedgehog. "Mrs. Tiggy as a model is comical." "The hedgehog drawings are turning out very comical." Mrs. Tiggy and Kitty seem both to have been persistently "comical."

After reading the journal and rereading her books, one feels a tenderness and admiration for Beatrix Potter that is difficult to express and should perhaps be left unexpressed for fear of sentimentalizing an emphatically unsentimental lady. On the subject of her art and of all matters that touched her deeply, Beatrix Potter typically chose to express herself humorously, ironically, with restraint; she gently mocked everyone's enthusiasms, especially her own. She could thus satirize one of her own passions, the study of fungi: "He [G. Massee, a principal assistant at the Herbarium] was growing funguses in little glass covers, and, being carried away by his subject, confided that one of them had spores three inches long. I opine that he has passed several stages of development into a fungus himself—I am occasionally conscious of a similar transformation."

[*1966*]

Beatrix Potter / 2

Not long ago I discussed children's books with some colleagues before an audience of intense and deeply concerned parents. From the outset, we on the panel made an effort to qualify our position as experts on children's literature; we all felt the distastefulness of being dubbed "experts." But these parents were full of complaints about the books being published for their children, and they seemed to feel that the members of the panel should agree with their complaints and do something about them.

Their concern, as it turned out, was due in large measure to what they considered a lack of seriousness and a proper attitude on the part of the artists and writers now creating books for children. Some other day I might have a few things to say about that complaint, but today I want to tell you about another one that was registered that evening. A gentleman in the audience raised his hand and with a voice full of righteous fervor declared that no one on the panel had as yet explained how a book as simpleminded and flat

[*This paper was delivered to a group of librarians and educators in New York City in June 1965*]

as *Peter Rabbit* deserved its prestigious reputation. Worst of all, it seemed to him to be "neither fact nor even fancy." To my horror, there were some murmurs of approval and even applause. I was speechless with indignation. How does one respond to such a sacrilege, except with the natural reply: "Well, if you can't see!"? But apparently there are those who can't. What, after all, has *Peter Rabbit* to do with "the problems confronting our children in today's tangled world"?

It is true that *Peter Rabbit* cannot be used as a handbook for the care and feeding of rabbits, nor can it be easily defined as a fantasy. If poor *Peter Rabbit* doesn't fit into any of these departments, what is all the noise about? At least that is the question the gentleman in the audience seemed to be asking. The answer, of course, is "Nothing," if one insists on breaking a work of art into bits and pieces for the empty satisfaction of forcing it into some pigeon-hole, a pastime for the unimaginative and the philistine alike.

We working artists on the panel made very plain the pointlessness of assigning this or that book to this or that pigeonhole. And that just added to the confusion. We agreed among ourselves that, in spite of the differences between the fact book and the fantasy book, *both* should properly come under the heading (if we must have a heading) of imaginative writing. We even agreed that many of the dead objects passing as books today might have been created by misguided artists, the sort who attempt to fit their work into meaningless pigeonholes under the illusion that factual truth and fictional truth have nothing to do with each other.

It is just here that *I* find confusion. The differences between a tale of fantasy and a factual account are self-evident, but I wonder if those of us concerned with books for the young sufficiently recognize that *any* life-enhancing book is more or less a product of the imagination. I don't mean imagination limited to conjuring up make-believe worlds, but rather an imagination which contributes a sense of life to all worlds, factual and fantastical. To outlaw imagination in any book on the grounds that it is synonymous with fantasy and has nothing to do with a down-to-earth account of, say, the principles of the automobile engine is to distort the meaning of "imagination" and produce the lifeless.

But I have strayed far from the panel discussion. I think we made it quite clear that there were no oracles seated on the platform that evening. However, for all our efforts, we were treated as experts and not too subtly condemned for being not-too-expert experts. But I don't mind being discredited for failing to care that *Peter Rabbit* is neither fish nor fowl, for being glad, in fact, that this work of the imagination defies pigeonholing.

That gentleman in the audience contended that the people inhabiting "the world of children's books" had foisted *Peter Rabbit* onto the public. He, for one, resented that. He saw through the lie; in a word, he saw nothing. What had that silly rabbit to do with the hard facts of life, or even the dream facts? Where was the imagination? Alas, I could not find the words to defend Peter to the gentleman in the audience. How does one defend the obvious? My only impulse was to smash him in the nose. *That* would be defending the honor of Beatrix Potter. Being aware, however, even from the platform, that his height and breadth were greater than my own, I quietly sulked instead. But here, in front of sympathetic and no doubt true-blue Potterites, I can bravely state my case: *Peter Rabbit* transcends all arbitrary categories. It is obviously no more a fact book about the habits of rabbits than it is a purely fantastical tale. It demonstrates that fantasy cannot be completely divorced from what is real; that fantasy heightens and contributes new insights into that reality.

I know that *Peter Rabbit*, for this audience, needs no boosting from me, but I would like to point to a few details that might help make my own feelings about it clear. I will refer, of course, to both words and pictures, for in this book there is no separating them.

Above all, this tiny book vividly communicates a sense of life, and this, I believe, is achieved through an imaginative synthesis of factual and fantastical components. Amazingly, Peter is both endearing little boy and expertly drawn rabbit. In one picture he stands most unrabbitlike, crying pitifully when there seems no way out of his dilemma. In another he bounds, leaving jacket behind, in a delightful rabbit bound, most unboylike, proving what we already know from her published sketchbooks: that Beatrix Potter drew from careful observation of her subject. And how she could draw!—a gift not all illustrators are endowed with.

This book, so apparently simple, smooth, straight-forward, is to my eye textured and deepened by the intimate, humorous observations that Beatrix Potter makes in her pictures. Take the birds, for example, that emotionally mirror the action. Flopsy, Mopsy, and Cottontail, the good little bunnies, are accompanied by two chipper, pecking birds whose routine busyness seems to represent the humdrum behavior of those cautious three. On the other hand, the bird observing Peter on his dangerous mission has an air of still, sorrowful speculation. He represents, I imagine, the helplessness and concern we feel for Peter. He seems ancient and philosophic in his doomlike observation of

Peter's shoe under the cabbage; I can almost see him shake his head. There is nothing chirpy about him. His movements are as quiet as the deadly atmosphere that hangs over Mr. McGregor's garden. But there is no mention of birds in the text until much later, when Peter, trapped in the gooseberry net, is implored by three sparrows "to exert himself." And what a brilliant threesome! There is such beauty in the drawing, and it is so convincing, that their passionate outcry is almost audible. Peter does exert himself, and escapes in the nick of time from Mr. McGregor's dreadful sieve; and the three sparrows, who surely could have flown away long before, have stopped with Peter up to the last moment, and all burst off to freedom together. They are apparently the same three who, near the end of the tale, anxiously watch Peter slip underneath the gate into the safety of the wood outside the garden; three birds who, in Peter's presence, behave almost like guiding spirits. Flopsy, Mopsy, and Cottontail attract only garden-variety birds.

I tremendously admire the poetry of Miss Potter's art as she develops this fantastic, realistic, truthful story. There is Peter pathetically slumped against the locked door in the wall; and there is the old mouse, her mouth too full of a large pea to answer Peter's desperate inquiry as to the way to the gate and freedom. She can only shake her head at him, and he can only cry. This tiny scene has the exact quality of nightmare: the sense of being trapped and frightened and finding the rest of the world (in this case, an old mouse) too busy keeping itself alive to help save you.

And last, I recall my favorite scene of the white cat, that lovely creature so prettily painted in the sylvan setting of Mr. McGregor's garden. How fortunate her back is turned to Peter, who very wisely thinks "it best to go away without speaking to her; he had heard

about cats from his cousin, little Benjamin Bunny."
What a typical Beatrix Potter understatement! For me,
this picture marvelously blends opposing images: the
sweet surface charm of the delicate watercolor garden
dominated by an innocent-looking cat who, on closer
observation, turns out to be fearful in color; that is, its
innocent whiteness becomes a dreadful *absence* of
color. The taut, twitching tail and the murderous
tension of muscle under the plump, firm exterior
betray the untamable cat nature. The poor witless
goldfish in the pond at its feet haven't got a chance.

I have tried to suggest the kind of imaginative blend
of fact and fantasy, integrated and working together
harmoniously, that creates for me the aliveness of
Peter Rabbit. Fantasy, rooted in the living fact: here,
the fact of family, of fun, of danger and fear; of the
evanescence of life; and finally, of safety, of mother
and love. Altogether the book possesses, on no matter
how miniature a scale, an overwhelming sense of life,
and isn't that the ultimate value of any work of art?
This standard should be applied to every book for the
young, and no book can claim the distinction of art
without it. *Peter Rabbit*, for all its gentle tininess,
loudly proclaims that no story is worth the writing,
no picture worth the making, if it is not a work of
imagination.

[*1965*]

Winsor McCay

When Pop Art breached the walls of academic snobbery, it made possible the rediscovery of some of our best popular culture. Winsor McCay, for example, the creator of *Little Nemo in Slumberland*, has begun to receive the recognition he deserves. *Little Nemo* is a comic strip—but much more than a comic strip, especially in comparison to the debased examples of the form popular in America since the late thirties. It is an elaborate and audacious fantasy that suffers only slightly from the cramped space imposed by its form. It is, in effect, a giant children's book, though no more limited to children than *Alice in Wonderland* or the Grimm tales.

Until some months ago I had never really read *Little Nemo*'s text. I had responded to its visual images and had invented my own *Nemo* by reading between these "lines" and absorbing what suited me. My *Nemo* goes back a long way (the numerous histories of the comics published in the forties and fifties showed tantalizing sample pages), but it wasn't until 1966, at a Metropolitan Museum exhibit entitled "Two Fantastic Draftsmen," that I saw the actual *Little Nemo*, in original size and full color. I realized finally what up until then I had only dimly felt: McCay and I serve the same master, our child selves. We both draw not on the literal memory of childhood but on the emotional memory of its stress and urgency. And neither of us forgot our childhood dreams.

Little Nemo is a catalogue of nightmares, a profusion of extreme fantasy images rendered with such explicit definition that the dream is captured in all its surrealistic exactitude. There are many details that I suspect only children see, and those few adults who still look with a child's intelligent curiosity. McCay's theme is the fantasy of escape to "some other place," away from confusion and pain, a flight from ambivalent parents. It is easy to deduce this without actually reading the words. For years I had devoured only the images and understood them by instinct. In a sense, I had extracted the *Nemo* Id and overlooked its Superego, for McCay's text is often a calculated front for the primal antics of his hero.

Little Nemo in Slumberland began as a full-page Sunday comic in the *New York Herald* on October 15, 1905, appeared there through July 23, 1911, and then moved to Hearst's *New York American* under the title *In the Land of Wonderful Dreams*. The strip was published in the *American* and a number of other newspapers until 1913, and McCay revived it from 1924 to 1926. Throughout this history, the formula remained the same. Nemo sleeps, dreams, and, in the last panel, wakes up. (McCay wryly suggests sardines or something else Nemo ate before bed as the reason for his dreams.) When the dreams are nightmares, which they mostly are, Nemo wakes up screaming or falls out of bed. On the few occasions when they are peaceful, he has to be roughly waked up.

The strange characters who inhabit Nemo's dreams, and the astonishing landscapes that contain them, have a ruggedness and vitality derived in part from McCay's theatrical experience. McCay was born in Michigan, the son of a lumberjack, in 1869. In adolescence he traveled with a Wild West show, doing odd jobs. He studied drawing in his home state, but his wish to continue at Chicago's Art Institute was dropped because he had to earn a living. In 1889 he joined a traveling carnival as official billboard painter and then became poster artist for the Cincinnati Dime Museum—actually, a freak show. In 1900 he became staff artist for the *Cincinnati Enquirer*, and in 1904 his genius finally found itself in a series of comic strips: *Dream of the Rarebit Fiend* for the *New York Evening Telegram*; and for the *New York Herald*, *The Story of Hungry Henrietta* and the superb *Little Sammy Sneeze*.

By 1905, when Nemo was born, Winsor McCay had become master of the form, a master who was self-taught: "The principal factor in my success has been an absolute desire to draw constantly. I never decided to be an artist. Simply, I couldn't stop myself from drawing. I drew for my own pleasure. I never wanted to know whether or not someone liked my drawings. I have never kept one of my drawings. I drew on walls, the school blackboard, odd bits of paper, the walls of barns. Today I'm still as fond of drawing as when I was a kid—and that's a long time ago—but, surprising as it may seem, I never thought about the money I would receive for my drawings. I simply drew them." (I am indebted to Judith O'Sullivan, research fellow at the National Collection of Fine Arts, for all the biographical data included here.)

McCay's mature style reflects the carnival poster's demand for vivid, clear shapes and showy motifs. The grandiose façades, the freaks, clowns, fancily tricked-out dancers, and comic-mirror distortions became the raw material from which he fashioned Nemo's world. All that and Art Nouveau, too.

In 1904 Alphonse Mucha had established a studio in New York and no doubt this interested McCay. "I think it would be wise for every art student to set up a certain popular artist whom he likes best and adapt his 'handling' or style. You don't have to copy his drawings, but when you are puzzled with any part of your work, see how it has been handled by your favorite and fix it up in a similar manner." McCay was as good as his word. He injected new spirit into the agitated, voluptuous line and arbitrary, flat-color patterning of Art Nouveau.

His originality is confirmed by his innovative method of visual narrative (he ignored the comic strip's traditional arrangement of panels, stretched them vertically and horizontally to get his dreamlike effects) and a radically personal iconography. McCay was a born architect with a breathtaking command of perspective; the elaborate structural decors that appear over and over in *Nemo* are reminiscent of the architectural fantasies of the stage designers of the Baroque. The power of his visionary landscapes, the strength of his draftsmanship override and mitigate the softening Art Nouveau conceits he enthusiastically took up.

Slumberland abounds in exotic birds, looped lilies, trailing flora, and asexual mermaids. Small matter. *Little Nemo* is nearly pure gold. If it falters now and again—and, at the end, repeatedly—it is impressive that McCay could sustain his creation at such an exalted level while producing a color comic page every week. But then, he loved to draw, and the promise of frequent escape into his child-hero's dreams must have been a helpful impetus.

The best of *Little Nemo* is sufficient proof that Mc-

Cay was one of America's rare, great fantasists. In a country that is ambivalent, at best, toward its volatile imaginations, further proof of his power is the fact that he could hold a mass audience for so long. Miraculously, McCay re-created dreams that we all had as children but few of us remember—or care to remember. This puts him squarely in league with Lewis Carroll and George MacDonald. Nemo's dreams, like Alice's, have the unquestionable ring of truth. In Slumberland, as in Wonderland, irrational taboos, forbidden places, and terrifying creatures confront our hero at every turn. But Nemo, unlike Alice, is afraid. He has none of her nimble wit and maddening pugnaciousness. He is dubious, suspicious, very much a miniature Buster Keaton ogling a hostile universe.

Nemo has good reason for his caution. The Slumberland refrain ("This is the most beautiful place you ever saw—you'll like it, Nemo!") is so much hogwash. Almost always, fun and games end in disaster. Nemo turns party pooper. He is passive, hesitates, and lets Flip, his fiery, aggressive friend-adversary, run the show. Nemo lacks savoir faire. He's as naïve and American as apple pie.

In the strip's first episodes, the basic themes are struck. The Princess of Slumberland longs for a playmate, and Nemo is her choice. He is conducted to her by a series of oddly named, lavishly costumed messengers, but, typically, it is a journey plagued with anxiety and frustration. Nemo doesn't meet the (understandably) near-crazed Princess until March 4, 1906! Besides the motive of suspense, I suspect another cause for the delay.

The Princess is almost characterless, a glossy, fortyish-looking, Klimt type; and she is often very badly drawn—something so rare for McCay it must be

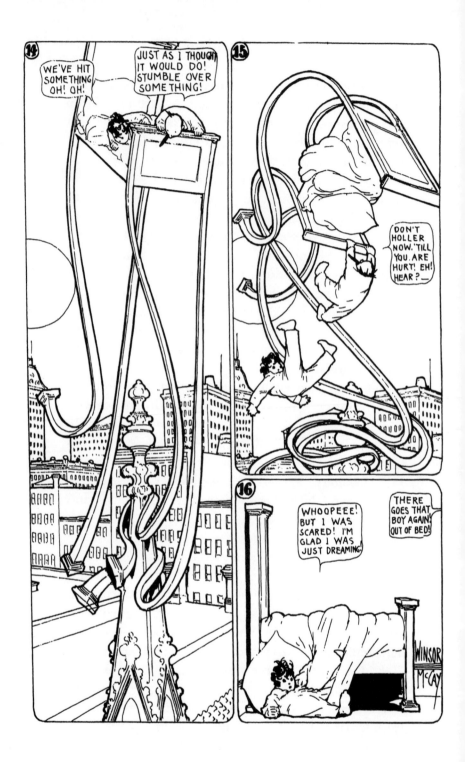

WINSOR MCCAY / *Detail from Little Nemo in Slumberland*

significant. Slumberland, unlike Wonderland, is a male-dominated society and the Princess is its token female, the only female in the regular cast. Nemo links up here with Captain Ahab and Huck Finn in the great American flight from women. Despite all talk to the contrary, he is not altogether satisfied with his princess; he'd much rather be out with the boys.

Toward the end of 1907 the Princess is temporarily dropped, and immediately the action picks up. Nemo, Flip, and the cannibal child, Imp, have a raucous, harum-scarum time away from the restraints of Slumberland. The fantasy flowers into one of the finest *Nemo* episodes, "Befuddle Hall," and Nemo's character develops as well. At the beginning of 1908 the boys are lost—they obviously want to be lost—and the change in our hero becomes significant. An unprecedented concern with social wrongs crops up in the "Shanty Town" episode (beginning March 22, 1908), when Nemo assumes a Christ-like role and restores a dying child to life. But in spite of the Dickensian tone (sick little sister Mary), this drama is cloying.

I'd imagine that McCay was thoroughly tired of Slumberland by 1908; its rigid formalities, red tape, and stuffy social procedures were alarming, like everyday life. After that summer, Slumberland is hauled in halfheartedly now and again, and finally, in 1910, though frequently mentioned afterward, it is dropped.

The best *Little Nemo* pages, in terms of imaginative leaps, are the early ones. As time went on, *Nemo* tended to become a serial, a fantasy chopped into weekly installments. In 1909 there are some curiously sadistic episodes. McCay is in a strange mood, and out of that mood Nemo suddenly turns fierce and aggressive and physically challenges Flip. They fight and Nemo wins. A sad victory: Nemo exchanges childhood for manhood, never thinking he might have both. After that, no matter how difficult the situation, Nemo is manfully optimistic and finally a little bullheaded and domineering. McCay, I'd venture a guess, had come through a crisis. The echo of that personal battle reverberates throughout Slumberland.

Now Nemo's adventures take a new turn. On a tour of the universe, we are granted a chilling look into the future. McCay anticipates our present problems: pollution of the environment, destruction of natural resources, overpopulation. The citizens of Mars are tyrannized by large corporations, and freedom is bestowed only on those who can afford to pay for it. Over the archway to the doomed planet are the bleak words: "Abandon hope, all ye who try to enter here without the price." It is the anti-human world of today. The final adventure in this collection is a grand tour of the United States and Canada, a spectacular farewell. Here McCay indulges his lifelong interest in reportorial drawing, and the views of Yellowstone, Niagara Falls, and, best of all, the Brooklyn Bridge are dazzling.

But this is another *Nemo*; fantasy has merged with reality and is lost forever. Slumberland has vanished and so has childhood. It seems to be a particularly American equation that manhood spells the death of childhood. I wish McCay had believed in Blake's joyful vision of imagination as the child in man. Little Nemo, by the end of 1910, though still little, is nothing more than a midget Teddy Roosevelt, impeccably dressed in Rough Rider uniform and issuing orders. The Superego in full swing.

The anthology published by Nostalgia Press presents the *New York Herald Little Nemo*, with some omissions, from the beginning in 1905 through December 25, 1910. Two hundred and sixty-three pages are reproduced, over one hundred of them in color as true to the originals as the Italian printers could manage. The reproductions measure approximately ten by thirteen inches, two-thirds the original size and large enough for the finest details to be preserved. It is a magnificent book, and all the credit for its existence belongs to Woody Gelman, collector, editor, and the best friend Winsor McCay ever had. It is an ironic fact that this collection of McCay's most important work had to be published in Italy first. America, it seems, still doesn't take its great fantasists all that seriously.

[1973]

Maxfield Parrish

I first saw Maxfield Parrish's pictures in Kenneth Grahame's two books about children—often mistaken for children's books—*Dream Days* and *The Golden Age*, illustrated respectively in 1898 and 1899. These pictures combine Parrish's then favorite techniques, wash, line, and stipple. Early printings of the books were shot in halftone and consequently lost all of Parrish's subtle shadings. The photogravure process used in later editions gives a better accounting of the illustrations. Their photographic surrealism combines fact and fancy in a meticulously depicted dream world. Parrish adds the depth and mystery that are missing from Grahame's charming but chilly stories. I love these pictures. Even if Parrish had done no other illustrations, these pages would secure him a place among America's few great fantasists. Happily for all of us, he did many more.

His first illustrated book, L. Frank Baum's *Mother Goose in Prose* (1897), already had the extraordinary Parrish qualities. Overflowing with good humor and imagination, these fine drawings in line and stipple offer elegantly patterned shapes and shrewdly composed blank areas. Parrish knew well the value of white space. His Baum pictures reveal a completely original vision that adds an otherworldly dimension to the book. *Mother Goose in Prose* launched his career and made Parrish famous.

Between the Baum and his last and best illustrated book, *The Knave of Hearts* (1925), Parrish illustrated the work of a remarkable assortment of writers. Among his most important books were Edith Wharton's *Italian Villas* (1904), Eugene Field's *Poems of Childhood* (1904), *The Arabian Nights* (1909), and Hawthorne's *A Wonder Book and Tanglewood Tales* (1910). The twenty-six illustrations in *Italian Villas* attest to Parrish's lasting interest in architecture, a youthful aspiration that was never fulfilled. Perhaps the most important features of the children's books are the stylistic and thematic elements introduced earlier and now expanded and more fully developed. His fascination with geometric patterns, folded and draped fabrics, and the famous Parrish blue sky was clearly defined in these works. The pictures are more fanciful and decorative than deeply concerned with the texts.

His last illustrated work, *The Knave of Hearts* by Louise Saunders, is his masterpiece. It is an oversized, overwhelming book in spectacular color. Parrish's romantic themes are juxtaposed here with his medieval and classical conceits (maidens and youths costumed commedia dell'arte fashion), all gloriously staged in a fabulist's landscape. It is not so much an illustrated book (the text is not worthy of him) as it is a celebration of the best of Maxfield Parrish.

As an important contributor to turn-of-the-century poster art, Parrish retained many images from his children's books. Most notable are his grotesque goblin figures and his penchant for structures of oddly mixed architectural styles. He won a number of national poster contests, the most important of them sponsored by *Century* magazine in 1897. One of the most famous of all Parrish images, the prize winner depicts a nude girl seated on the grass, gazing off into the sky.

One cannot help comparing Parrish with Winsor McCay, the creator of *Little Nemo in Slumberland.* McCay was more noticeably influenced by Art Nouveau's sensuous, curvilinear forms, but their palettes were somewhat similar. More to the point, both artists were remarkable draftsmen who energetically and successfully mixed fantasy and reality to create a private world that, for all its strangeness, is precisely rendered.

Parrish and McCay share many faults as well, among them an unfortunate weakness for soft, languid, sexually neuter types, picked up in Parrish's case from the vapid imagery of the Pre-Raphaelites, and in McCay's from the swoonings of Art Nouveau. It is a tendency that represents, to my mind, a false, sentimentalizing, anti-sexual notion about childhood that has a damaging effect on their work. It is a curious fact that America, usually so hostile to its dream-driven artists, took such a fancy to these two— at least, for a time. This phenomenon might have something to do with our odd, antiquated, Peter Pan view of childhood: a doctored memory of childhood evoked so romantically, so nostalgically by Parrish and, to a lesser extent, by McCay. Parrish's creatures live in a presexual Eden. Robust sexuality was the dark cloud that never tainted the heavenly blue of a Parrish sky. And McCay's Nemo, when he was allowed to grow up, traded the best of childhood for the worst of manhood.

Parrish was certainly the most popular artist of post-World War I America. This was a time when the popular arts were still in lively communication with the fine, and a kind of give-and-take refreshed and deepened both. It was a happy time, before "commercial art" became a term of opprobrium, and before the myth flourished that the achievement of popular success in the arts exiled one from the realm of the serious. This is a form of snobbery that would have been incomprehensible to Parrish (or Winslow Homer, for that matter). In an interview in 1931, Parrish said: "I'm done with girls on rocks. I have painted them for thirteen years and I could paint and sell them for thirteen more. That is the peril of the commercial-art game. It tempts a man to repeat himself." Thereafter, most of his paintings were landscapes. If Parrish had hopes of quitting "the commercial-art game," he must have been cruelly disappointed. The Brown and Bigelow Publishing Company used his "personal" landscapes on more than seven and a half million calendars, three million greeting cards, and one million prints. (A suitable epitaph for poor Parrish might have been: If you're successful, you just can't win.)

Is his work high art? No, but Parrish never aspired to the level of Eakins and Homer. Their concerns were not his, and we ought not to judge him as if they were. His technical proficiency can mislead us. He was a popular artist in the best sense of the word. Supremely capable of meeting the demands of art for mass consumption, he never sacrificed his personal standards.

If Parrish has, at the moment, been taken up too noisily for fashionable reasons (my bathroom is adorned with an old print of his "Daybreak," that ultra-kitsch favorite of two neuter nudes on a portico against a background of too-blue mountains, in its original garish frame), this will pass. His work, like all popular art, exists parallel to the world of fine arts, and Pop and Op have encouraged us to reassess the masters of the popular form.

Maxfield Parrish was a modest man who once said of himself: "I am hopelessly commonplace." Perhaps, but the commonplace transfigured.

[*1974*]

Claud Lovat Fraser

I discovered *Peacock Pie* when I jostled a shelf at the Argosy Book Shop in 1958. The book fell on my head. No one had prepared me for Lovat Fraser, and I'm grateful for that. As in the case of another favorite, Arthur Hughes, I had the profound pleasure of finding him by myself, as well as the good sense to be influenced by his work and to collect thereafter everything by him I could lay my hands on.

I have borrowed borders from Fraser, and the lovely, squared, fresh-colored look he often gave a design. But he has something far more important than mere style to excite my eclectic tastes. His work embodies a point of view that is worth noting and incorporating into one's creative psyche. He was free of aesthetic snobbery. With the same care and integrity, with relish and joy that are altogether beguiling, he embellished, decorated, and designed everything from charming ephemera to his glorious stage productions. No form was beneath him.

As an illustrator, I inevitably admire him most for his books. Behind the deceptively casual style is an astonishing purity of design and richness of invention.

Fraser the illustrator was a particularly great virtuoso, without ostentation or self-consciousness. His books convey a curious happiness; one loves the man through the work.

It is sad how little his contribution to modern book illustration is acknowledged. His influence on my own work—my attitude toward my work—has been considerable. It was a lucky bump on the head that brought me to Lovat Fraser.

[*1971*]

Jean de Brunhoff

Babar's escape to Paris, when he fled the jungle in 1931, was not, alas, via Brooklyn. If he had come my way, how I would have welcomed that orphaned little elephant and smothered him with affection. What a pity he didn't visit my house. Some of that gentle spirit, those sensible ways, might have rubbed off on a child whose childhood was largely governed by ungoverned emotions. When I did make his acquaintance, as a young artist in the early 1950s, it was too late. By then, raised on a diet of Sturm und Drang, I inwardly condemned the Babar books for what I considered an overly reasoned approach to life: typically French, I said then. About this last judgment I was right, but not in my negative inference. So, although I admired the whole series of books, their Gallic tone, which I interpreted as aloofness, continued to rankle. And while I loved the Babars, I loved them primarily for their graphic splendor.

After all, the French, at the turn of the century, had practically reinvented the illustrated book. Along with the work of André Hellé, Edy Legrand, Maurice Boutet de Monvel, Félix Vallotton, and Pierre Bonnard, Jean de Brunhoff's picture books have a freedom and charm, a freshness of vision, that captivates and takes the breath away. Like a virtuoso poetic form, the interplay between few words and many pictures commonly called the picture book makes aesthetic demands that few have mastered. The best examples should rightfully take their place with comparably sophisticated "grownup" works of art.

Jean de Brunhoff was a master of this form. Between 1931 and 1937 he completed a body of work that forever changed the face of the illustrated book. Undoubtedly, he had no such ambition. Like William Nicholson, who created two of England's best picture books, *Clever Bill* and *The Pirate Twins*, to amuse his children, de Brunhoff, inspired by his wife and young sons, created Babar.

Jean de Brunhoff was born in 1899. His father, Maurice, a Frenchman of Baltic and Swedish origins, was a publisher of art magazines, among them the very elegant *Program of Serge Diaghilev's Ballets Russes*. Jean, in fact, came from a family of publishers; his brother Michel was editor-in-chief of the French *Vogue* and his brother-in-law Lucien Vogel published the fashion magazine *Le Jardin des Modes* and later *Vu*. Jean was a painter who put himself somewhere on the edge of the avant-garde stream. In 1924 he married Cécile Sabouraud, a pianist, and it is forever to her credit that one day in 1931 she invented the story of a little elephant to amuse the two young de Brunhoff children, Mathieu and Laurent. The children enthusiastically related the story to their papa, and thus began Babar.

My early indifference to de Brunhoff's writing was, in retrospect, a curious and significant blind spot. I was busy then, furiously learning what a picture book was and, more to the point, what it could be. That learning consisted mostly of swooping, magpie-like, into the works of Randolph Caldecott, Beatrix Potter, William Nicholson, and Edward Ardizzone and taking away what most suited my creative purposes. This was in the 1950s. I was then a green recruit fresh from the analyst's couch and woe betide any work that failed to loudly signal its Freudian allegiance. With a convert's proverbial fervor, I rushed pell-mell into the very heart of what I considered Babar's unresolved problem: his mother's death, of course.

I never quite got over that death. The ease and remarkable calm with which de Brunhoff blighted the life of his baby elephant numbed me. That sublimely happy babyhood lost after only two pictures! Then, as in a nightmare (and too much like life), Babar, cruelly and arbitrarily deprived of his loving mother, runs wildly out of babyhood (the innocent jungle) and into cozy, amnesia-inducing society (Paris, only blocks away from that jungle). It is there that he feverishly embraces adulthood, culture, manners, any distraction, to forget the hideous trauma of that useless death. Or so it seemed to me then. Why give us a mother's death and then deprive us of the pleasure of wallowing in its psychological repercussions? Why not, in fact, go back and find another, less volatile reason for Babar to flee the jungle? Easy enough solution, thought I. In summation, I judged this death to be a gratuitously punishing touch, an issue raised and bewilderingly passed over. Somehow I missed the point. It took years of further exposure to the work of many different artists, my own redefinition of the picture-book form, and much growing up to complete my appreciation of Babar. Now, from a distance of more than thirty years, I see that Babar is at the very heart of my conception of what turns a picture book into a work of art. The graphics are tightly linked to the "loose" prose-poetry, remarkable for its ease of expression. The pictures, rather than merely echoing the words, enrich and expand Babar's world.

Laurent de Brunhoff, Jean's eldest son, and I are colleagues and old, good friends. In large part, it is Laurent who urged me out of my frantic Freudian "dig," without ever denying the existence of those significant clues in Jean's Babar. He helped adjust my extremist view of his father's work to a more moderated, clear-cut understanding.

In the summer of 1977 Laurent invited me to his family home. We took the train at Gare St.-Lazare to the small village of Epône and then walked a memorable two miles through the Seine Valley to his house. It is an old, rather plain stone villa surrounded by a high wall and covered with ivy. Marie-Claude and Anne, Laurent's wife and daughter, were there to greet me. In the garden I met Mme Jean de Brunhoff, a handsome, youthful-looking woman in her seventies, and Laurent's youngest brother, Thierry. I remember the comfortable quiet, a stalking cat named Ursule, and a three-mile hike through wheat fields, poppies, and roses, with the Seine always in view. It was that relaxed quiet that impressed me most—not an isolating, disconcerting stillness, but rather the sun and peace of a good Sunday in the country. One breathed in the sense of privacy and family and it felt very good. If I linger on this episode, it is because it so sharply registers on my mind's eye as I reread Babar. This ordered, tight-knit feeling of family is the essence of Babar. It may be foolish to say that my day with the de Brunhoffs helped me to find my Babar bearings, but it is something like the truth.

Jean de Brunhoff, it seems, had to be oblique. Perhaps he knew, instinctively, what I was to learn, that this was the best way to reach and teach children. Beneath the zaniness, the originality of style, and the vivacity of imagination is a serious and touching theme: a father writing to his sons and voicing his natural concern for their welfare, for their lives. At the end of *Babar and His Children*, King Babar says, "Truly it is not easy to bring up a family." And truly it is this hard wisdom that lies at the heart of the books. Why was this such a vital issue in the creation of Babar? In the early 1930s, Jean de Brunhoff contracted tuberculosis. Bettina Hürlimann, in her excellent *Three Centuries of Children's Books in Europe*, strongly suggests that, had he not been suffering from this disease, there might never have been a Babar. She implies that the books were written by a dying young father, far from his children, as his only means of staying in touch with them. Laurent's memories disagree. He recalls much time spent *en famille*, "winter months in the mountains, summer months in the country, and in between in Paris." He recalls, too, his father's naturally "humorous and gentle view of people and things." That Jean had intimations of death must be true. That he was a loving, generous-spirited man is true, too. We see it in his work. And, in my many conversations with Laurent, it has been clear that Jean never communicated to his children the private fears and regrets he surely had. He died in 1937. Laurent was twelve at the time and Thierry, the youngest, was not yet three. Jean's bequest to his family, and the world, shines from the books that rushed from his pen at the extraordinary rate of almost one a year between 1931 and 1937. These contain, in Hürlimann's words, "glimpses of things dear to the de Brunhoff family as the background for a father's affectionate counsel"—his counsel on coming of age with grace and kindness, on weathering the inevitable storms of life.

The devotion to family and the circumstances of life

that produced Babar must account for the special power and honest sentiment that are the essence of de Brunhoff's work. These considerations also help to explain the balanced emotional climate that is never allowed to go out of control. And here I come back to my first appraisal of Babar, but in a new, most sympathetic light. These books are so traditionally French, filled with what might be considered old-fashioned ideas of manhood, womanhood, and manners. But there is always an underlying emphasis on developing a child's (an elephant child's) personal freedom and individuality through self-control. Not self-control in the repressive sense, but defined rather as the awareness of choices of behavior, the awareness that some choices are better than others. "Do you see how in this life one must never be discouraged?" says *la Vieille Dame.* "Let's work hard and cheerfully and we'll continue to be happy." In *Babar the King,* an ordinary day suddenly turns into a nightmare. Babar is nearly overwhelmed by the arbitrary nature of disaster. But he is comforted by his dream, or vision, of graceful, winged elephants chasing Misfortune away from Celesteville and bringing back Happiness. Then he feels "ever so much better." He understands that it takes patience, with himself, and perseverance to be happy. It is an earned state of health.

My favorite among Jean's books, *The Travels of Babar,* is full of alarming and very amusing twists of fate. For the one and only time in all the books, Babar loses his fine balance and has a good old temper tantrum. He is brought out of it by Celeste. The two alternately comfort each other in times of stress. Here they resolve many crises and, with the good *Vieille Dame* in tow, rush to the mountains "to enjoy the fresh air and try a little skiing." At this point the book stops short so we can study, at leisure, the stupendous double spread of Babar, Celeste, and *la Vieille Dame* calmly gliding down the Swiss slopes. It is a picture filled with the intense concentration and pleasure of this favorite de Brunhoff sport.

Scale is crucial to de Brunhoff's pictures. Those first editions of Babar have an undiminished grandeur, with their huge, delectable format and spacious compositions. They are as pleasing to the eye and as totally original as anything coming out of that fine and rare period of French art. These early editions fell victim to the high cost of production and have been out of print for years. Children, sadly, can no longer "climb into" a Babar book.*

No one before and very few since have utilized the double-spread illustration to such dazzling, dramatic effect. When Babar and Celeste are taken prisoner in *The Travels of Babar*, there is a spectacular circus scene. The handsome red arch that denotes the arena floor is also a menacing symbol of their glittering confinement. There is no doubt that the artist is enjoying himself immensely. He has even placed himself in the scene, the young man sitting in the audience pedantically measuring Celeste for a portrait with his outstretched thumb and pencil. The line of text below the picture is so simple that the art absolutely "blooms" above the words. One can hear Babar's trumpet music. But these books are full of music, both literally and figuratively. The ravishing theater picture in *Babar the King*, with every element of architecture fancifully elephantized, is accompanied (at least for me) by the most delicious harpsichord music, Rameau perhaps. And were the grand parade scene from the same book to be set to a joyous march, Berlioz

---

Happily, since I wrote this, several of the Babar books have been re-issued in the original format.

Mais Babar est maintenant au cirque Fernando

et joue de la trompette pour faire danser Céleste

JEAN DE BRUNHOFF / *Le Voyage de Babar*

would be most suitable. This picture, by the way, actually moves rhythmically in step if you keep your eye on those stolid elephant feet, all thumpingly clumping to the same measure. Color, costume, high comedy mixed with touching solemnity blend into a characteristic composition that appears artless on the surface but is, in fact, extravagantly complex. And it makes a vivid psychological point. The celebration catches Babar, and all of Celesteville, at the very peak of happiness and security. Immediately following, and in a series of swift, comic-book-style squares, shockingly unlike the grandeur of the previous picture, we see the deterioration of that happiness: the near-death of *la Vieille Dame* from snakebite. The elephant world falls apart and only comes together again in the double spread of Babar's vision, and, not surprisingly, at the very end, when we are treated to a small version of that selfsame parade. It is still led by the blithe-spirited Zephir, this time carrying a flag with the motto "Long Live Happiness."

The little-known *Babar and His Children* is the most moving of the series. How happy Babar is to be the father of three little elephants! He knows well how to love his babies. After all, his own brief childhood was graced with the most intense and happy mother's love. And, like all wise elephants, Babar does not forget. He never forgets *la Vieille Dame* and he never forgets his mother. ("He often stands at the window, thinking sadly of his childhood, and cries when he remembers his mother.") Although Babar finds a sympathetic second mother in *la Vieille Dame*, this does not erase his early loss. That permeates all the books, but it is never allowed to overwhelm or destroy Babar's self-confidence. It is living that concerns and delights de Brunhoff. He recognizes death as inseparable from the fixed order of things and is never obsessed with it.

At this point I cannot resist quoting Laurent on the death of the old elephant king in *The Story of Babar*. "I do not want to be cynical," he said, "but he dies for the purpose of the plot, to make room for Babar! It is also done in a way to show death as a natural thing." How similar to the death of Babar's mother. How like de Brunhoff's own death, a natural occurrence moving the plot along.

The precious sense of reason that at first struck me as lack of feeling now moves and excites me. Babar, the "very good little elephant," deserves his kingdom. He is noble, certainly, and it is by proving this inner worth that he gains his position in life. But de Brunhoff's lessons are suggested in a tone at once so right and humorous, so engaging, that they are irresistible. The grace and graphic charm are almost sufficient by themselves, but to deny the message is to deny the full weight of Jean de Brunhoff's genius.

[*1981*]

Walt Disney / 1

This year, Mickey Mouse and I will be celebrating our fiftieth birthdays. We shared, at least for our first decade, much more than a first initial; it was the best of relationships and one of the few real joys of my childhood in Brooklyn during the early thirties.

Those were the Depression years and we had to make do. Making do—for kids, at least—was mostly a matter of comic books and movies. Mickey Mouse, unlike the great gaggle of child movie stars of that period, did not make me feel inferior. Perhaps it was typical for kids of my generation to suffer badly from unthinking parental comparisons with the then-famous silver-screen moppets. There is no forgetting the cheated, missed-luck look in my father's eyes as he turned from the radiant image of Shirley Temple back to the three ungolden children he'd begotten. Ah, the alluring American dream of owning a Shirley Temple girl and a Bobby Breen boy! I never forgave those yodeling, tap-dancing, brimming-with-glittering-life miniature monsters.

But Mickey Mouse had nothing to do with any of them. He was our buddy. My brother and sister and I chewed his gum, brushed our teeth with his toothbrush, played with him in a seemingly endless variety of games, and read about his adventures in comic strips and storybooks. Best of all, our street pal was also a movie star. In the darkened theater, the sudden flash of his brilliant, wild, joyful face—radiating great golden beams—filled me with an intoxicating, unalloyed pleasure.

In school, I learned to despise Walt Disney. I was told that he corrupted the fairy tale and that he was the personification of poor taste. I began to suspect my own instinctual response to Mickey. It took me nearly twenty years to rediscover the pleasure of that first response and to fuse it with my own work as an artist. It took me just as long to forget the corrupting effect of school.

Though I wasn't aware of it at the time, I now know that a good deal of my pleasure in Mickey had to do with his bizarre proportions: the great rounded head extended still farther by those black saucer ears, the black trunk fitting snugly into ballooning red shorts, the tiny legs stuffed into delicious doughy yellow shoes. The giant white gloves, yellow buttons, pie-cut eyes, and bewitching grin were the delectable finishing touches. I am describing, of course, the Mickey of early color cartoons (his first being *The Band Concert* of 1935). The black-and-white Mickey of the late twenties and early thirties had a wilder, rattier look. The golden age of Mickey for me is that of the middle thirties. A gratifying shape, fashioned primarily to facilitate the needs of the animator, he exuded a sense of physical satisfaction and pleasure—a piece of art that powerfully affected and stimulated the imagination.

I'm less a lover of Mickey's personality—the All-American Boy—than of his graphic image. (His provincialism disturbed me even as a child.) That golden-age Mickey metamorphosed, alas, into less original forms roughly at the end of his first decade. Every addition and modification to Mickey's proportions after that time was a mistake. He became a suburbanite, abandoning his street friends and turning into a shapeless, mindless bon vivant. Those subtle and sometimes not-so-subtle nuances pushed Mickey out of art into commerce. (Mickey, surely, was *always* commercial, but now he *looked* commercial.) This transformation, which I take so to heart, apparently made not a jot of difference to following generations. Mickey is as popular as ever. But those kids, like Mickey, were missing the best.

My own collection of Mickey Mousiana is rigidly bound by that first decade of his life. There is no end to such a collection, nor, oddly, is there any wish to end it. Happily and incredibly, there was an infinitude of Mouses manufactured in those early days (as there still is), and the search for an early Mouse becomes a delightful obsession. To seek out that face—that completely nuts look of fiery, intense animation—to find it on a postcard, box top, piece of tin or porcelain, is an enduring pleasure.

The Mickey who exerted influence on me as an artist is the Mickey of that early time—my early time. Playing a Kafka game of shared first initial with most of the heroes in my own picture books, I only once broke cover and fused a very particular character with the famous Mouse. That is the Mickey who is the hero of my picture book *In the Night Kitchen*. It seemed natural and honest to reach out openly to that early best friend while eagerly exploring a very private, favorite childhood fantasy. *In the Night Kitchen* is a kind of homage to old times and places—to Laurel and Hardy comedies and *King Kong*, as well as to the art of Disney, comic books in general, and the turn-of-the-century funny-papers fantasist Winsor McCay in particular. It was also an attempt to synthesize past and present, with Mickey as my trusty stand-in. And if the Disney studio irritatingly refused to let me paint his revered image on a cooking stove that figured in my plot, I put it down to the general decay of civilization.

Fifty is the notorious middle age of crisis and flux. But I have a fantasy of Mickey at this great age busting loose—à la Steamboat Willie—and declaring his independence by demanding back the original, idiosyncratic self that prosperity and indifference have robbed him of. Hardly likely, I suppose. But middle age has been known to precede a rebirth of spirit and inspiration, so maybe the Mouse has a chance.

[*1978*]

Walt Disney / 2

It is the winter of 1940. The world is five
months into a new war and I am very aware that it
is wrong to be happy. But I am. I have been prom-
ised a trip uptown to see Walt Disney's new film,
Pinocchio, and my only concern is not being late.
It is roughly an hour from Brooklyn to midtown
Manhattan on the BMT, and my sister and her girl-
friend are, as usual, dragging their feet. It is just another example of the awfulness of children's dependence on the adult world to fulfill their most desperate
wishes. By the time we reach the theater, I have lost
what little self-control I had left. The movie has already begun. I go into a black sulk and my sister, furious, threatens to abandon me altogether. We climb to
the balcony in angry silence and clamber across an invisible and endless row of knees to our seats. The
sound track, in the meantime, fills the dark with the
most irresistible music. I can't bear to look at the
screen. I have missed, I feel, the best of everything.
But my first glimpse once past the four thousandth
knee dissipates all my anguish. Jiminy Cricket is slid-
ing jauntily down the strings of a violin, singing "Give
a Little Whistle." (The scene occurs twenty minutes

into the film; I've clocked it often since that day.)
I was happy then and have remained forever happy
in the memory of *Pinocchio*.

If remembering that day is tinged with a confusing
guilt that has something to do with the inappropriate-
ness of feeling cheerful when a world war was hanging
over our heads, then that, too, is part of the precious
memory of *Pinocchio*. I was only a child, but I knew
something dreadful was happening in the world, and
that my parents were worried to death. And it seems
to me that something of the quality of that terrible,
anxious time is reflected in the very color and dramatic power of *Pinocchio*. Certainly, it is the darkest
of all Disney films. This is not to deny that it is also
a charming, amusing, and touching film. It is, however, rooted in melancholy, and in this respect it is
true to the original Italian tale. But that is where any
significant resemblance between Disney and Collodi
ends.

Disney has often been condemned for corrupting
the classics, and he has, to be sure, occasionally
slipped in matters of taste and absolute fidelity to
the original. But he has never corrupted. If there
have been errors, they are nothing compared to the
violations against the true nature and psychology of
children committed by some of the so-called classics.
C. Collodi's *Pinocchio*, first published in 1883, is a
case in point. As a child, I disliked it. When I grew
up, I wondered if perhaps my early dislike was ill
founded. My memory of the book was a mixture of
the utterly sad and the peculiarly unpleasant; and
when I finally reread it, I found that this memory
is accurate. While Collodi's *Pinocchio* is an undeniably engaging narrative that moves with tremendous
energy—despite its shaky, loose construction—it is
also a cruel and frightening tale. It does not suffer

from whimsicality or sentimentality, but its premise is sickening.

Children, Collodi appears to be saying, are inherently bad, and the world itself is a ruthless, joyless place, filled with hypocrites, liars, and cheats. Poor Pinocchio is *born* bad. While still mostly a block of firewood—just his head and hands are carved—he is already atrocious, instantly using those new hands to abuse his woodcarver papa, Geppetto. Only moments after Pinocchio's creation, Geppetto is wiping tears from his eyes and regretting the marionette's existence: "I should have thought of this before I made him. Now it is too late!" Pinocchio doesn't stand a chance; he is evil incarnate—a happy-go-lucky *ragazzo*, but damned nevertheless.

In order to grow into boyhood, Pinocchio has to yield up his own self entirely, unquestioningly, to his father—and, later in the book, to the strange lady with the azure hair (the Blue Fairy of the film). When that elusive lady promises to be Pinocchio's mother, there is this nasty hook attached: "You will obey me always and do as I wish?" Pinocchio promises that he will. She then delivers a dreary sermon, ending: "Laziness is a serious illness and one must cure it immediately; yes, even from early childhood. If not, it will kill you in the end." No wonder Pinocchio soon disobeys. His instincts warn him off and he runs away, apparently preferring laziness and wickedness to the castrating love of this hard-hearted fairy. It's a strange paradox that Collodi equates becoming "a real boy" with turning into a capon.

At its best, the book has moments of mad black humor, with more than a touch of Woody Allenish logic. When Pinocchio first meets the fairy, for instance, he is trying to escape from assassins who mean to rob and kill him. He knocks frantically on her door, and she appears at her window, with "a face white as wax," to tell him that everyone in the house, herself included, is dead. "Dead?" Pinocchio screams in fury. "What are you doing at the window, then?" That is Pinocchio's true voice. This hilarious, nightmarish scene ends with the exasperating lovely lady leaving the marionette to the mercy of the assassins—who hang him from a giant oak tree. The story is full of such ghastly, sadistic moments, most of them not funny at all.

So far as I am concerned, Collodi's book is of interest today chiefly as evidence of the superiority of Disney's screenplay. The Pinocchio in the film is not the unruly, sulking, vicious, devious (albeit still charming) marionette that Collodi created. Neither is he an innately evil, doomed-to-calamity child of sin. He is, rather, both lovable and loved. Therein lies Disney's triumph. His Pinocchio is a mischievous, innocent, and very naïve little wooden boy. What makes our anxiety over his fate endurable is a reassuring sense that Pinocchio is loved for himself—and not for what he should or shouldn't be. Disney has corrected a terrible wrong. Pinocchio, he says, is good; his "badness" is only a matter of inexperience.

Nor is Disney's Jiminy Cricket the boring, browbeating preacher/cricket he is in the book (so boring that even Pinocchio brains him). In the movie, we watch Jiminy's intelligent curiosity concerning the marionette quicken into genuine interest and affection. He is a loyal though not uncritical friend, and his flip and sassy ways do not diminish our faith in his reliability. Despite his failure to convince Pinocchio of the difference between right and wrong, his willingness to understand and forgive the puppet's foolish waywardness makes him a complicated cricket indeed. The Blue Fairy is still a bit stuffy about the virtues of truth and honesty, but she can laugh and is as quick as Jiminy to forgive. Who could fail to forgive inexperience?

Disney has deftly pulled the story together and made a tight dramatic structure out of the rambling sequence of events in the Collodi book. Pinocchio's wish to be a real boy remains the film's underlying theme, but "becoming a real boy" now signifies the wish to grow up, not the wish to be good. Our greatest fear is that he may not make his way safely through the minefields of his various adventures to get what, finally, he truly deserves. We still miss the little wooden boy at the end of the film (there is just no way of loving the flesh-and-blood boy as much as we did the marionette), but we are justifiably happy for Pinocchio. His wish to be a real boy is as passionate and believable a longing as is Dorothy's wish, in the film version of L. Frank Baum's *The Wizard of Oz*, to find her way home to Kansas. Both Pinocchio and Dorothy deserve to have their wishes come true; they prove themselves more than worthy. Oddly, both of these movies are superior to the "classics" that inspired them.

About two years were devoted to the production of *Pinocchio*, easily the best of the Disney films, as well as the most fearless and emotionally charged. Some 500,000 drawings appear on the screen, and this does not include tens of thousands of preliminary drawings, story sketches, atmosphere sketches, layouts, character models, and stage settings. Extensive use of the Disney-developed multi-plane camera—first tried out in *Snow White*—allows for ingenious camera movement similar to the dolly shots of live movie production. According to Christopher Finch in his book *The Art of Walt Disney*: "A single scene in which the multi-plane camera zooms down on the village with the school bells ringing and the pigeons circling down and down until they are among the houses cost $45,000 (equivalent to perhaps $200,000 today). The scene lasts only a few seconds . . . The result was an animated movie of unprecedented lavishness." The production details are overwhelming, but in the end they are only statistics. After half a century, the movie itself is the vital proof that all that manpower, machinery, and money went into creating a work of extraordinary skill, beauty, and mystery. And if there are flaws—and there are—the sheer force of originality easily compensates for them. If I wish the Blue Fairy didn't remind me of a typical thirties movie queen, and Cleo, the goldfish, of a miniature, underwater mix of Mae West and Carmen Miranda, this merely acknowledges that even masterpieces have their imperfections.

As for those tantalizing twenty minutes I missed back in February 1940, I have since seen them again and again, though that never makes up for missing them the first time. The movie contains so many memorable episodes; for example, the one in which Jiminy and Pinocchio converse in bubbling speech as they move about the ocean floor, looking for Monstro, the whale, and the swallowed Geppetto. And, near the end of the Pleasure Island sequence, there is the starkly terrifying scene in which Pinocchio's new friend, Lampwick, turns into a donkey. It starts amusingly enough, but Lampwick's growing alarm and then outright hysteria quickly become painful. His flailing arms turn into hoofs, and his last awful cry of *Ma-Ma*, as his shadow on the wall collapses onto all fours, makes us realize that he is lost forever.

After the dramatic ocean chase, when the vengeful Monstro tries to destroy Geppetto and Pinocchio, we see, with relief, the old woodcarver washed up on shore and Figaro, the cat, and Cleo in her bowl washed up beside him. A bedraggled Jiminy arrives next, calling for Pinocchio. Then the camera leaps to a shot of the marionette, face down in a pool of water: dead. That image, for me, is the most shocking in the whole film. Pinocchio has forfeited his life to save his father. Coming only moments later, in the funeral scene, is the Blue Fairy's reward. She revives the brave marionette into a new life as a real boy. Tactfully, we are not permitted to dwell too long on his ordinary, little boy's face.

Watching *Pinocchio* now, I am inevitably struck by a sense of regret—of loss. It would almost certainly be impossible to finance such an enterprise today. The movie has the golden glamour of a lost era; it is a monument to an age of craft and quality in America. It is too easy to shrug and say the money just isn't there anymore. In my own business of publishing, one watches with growing dismay the ersatz quality of bookmaking, the vanishing forever of traditional linotype faces, and the degeneration of paper. Over the past few decades, there has been a collapse of the sense of pride in craftsmanship, of the sense of excellence. Usually, this has nothing to do with money. A rough, early Mickey Mouse short—any one of them!—is superior to the animation that is currently manufactured for television. We are in the dark McDonald's age of the quick and easy. *Pinocchio* is a shining reminder of what once was—of what could be again.

[*1988*]

Edward Ardizzone

With easy aplomb, Edward Ardizzone has weathered the storms of fashionable style that have shipwrecked many talented but less sturdily dedicated illustrators. An artist whose work harks back to the great nineteenth-century watercolorists (and to the ingeniously constructed picture books of his country-man William Nicholson), Ardizzone has perpetuated the honorable tradition of English book illustration, adding sharp strokes of humor and insight that make all his work unusually fresh and immediate.

Published in America in 1936, his *Little Tim and the Brave Sea Captain* was the first of a series of comic but touching adventure stories that are classic studies in the mysterious art of picture-book making. From the beginning Ardizzone had an instinct for this most difficult form. He intuitively hit upon a formula for manipulating simple ingredients that results in a complexity and cohesion rarely achieved in picture books of this century.

Little Tim is an oversized, rowdy-looking book filled with robust, swiftly rendered watercolors that appear to have been casually, almost arbitrarily sketched around, under, and in and out of the text. Its large, loose, and easy look, maintained throughout the series, perfectly suits Tim's windswept, watery adventures and yet conceals architectonic elements—balance, pacing, pinpoint timing—that are basic to the picture book.

All the stories, with their inimitable touches of dry humor, are told in a poker-faced, mock-Victorian manner, and the dazzling watercolors and black-and-white sketches, dashed off in Ardizzone's very personal shorthand style, are frequently punctuated with funny asides voiced by the characters via balloons. The plots are almost ritualistic. There is always, of course, Tim, a proper, courageous, if somewhat headstrong seven-year-old who has an insatiable wanderlust and who lives in a house by the sea—so convenient for wanderlusting—with an astonishingly permissive and unrufflable mum and dad. Over the years Ardizzone has introduced such singular characters as Lucy, Charlotte (the odd mixture of almost Germanic whimsy and genteel poignancy makes *Tim and Charlotte* my favorite of the series), and Tim's mischievous friend Ginger.

Tim and Ginger, a tale of heroism, cowardice, and false accusation, is filled with delightfully predictable suspense but, unpredictably, falls short of the superlative standards maintained in the previous books. Perhaps a bit of underpinning shows, the formula plot seems somewhat strained, and the abbreviated style of the pictures borders on the careless. These defects, however, are of minor consequence, thanks to the buoyant, energetic, and very funny spirit that pervades all of Tim's adventures.

The action begins when Ginger scoffs at the old boatman's warning to beware of the treacherous tides while shrimping under the high chalk cliffs. "Poof!" says Ginger—who poofs loudly all through the book—

as he goes off shrimping. Needless to say, he doesn't come back and Tim, desperately worried, rows off to the rescue in a borrowed boat (which he is later accused of stealing). Just in time he saves Ginger, who "was in a terrible plight. By standing on the tips of his toes, he could only just keep his head above the sea. However, he was soon on board and seemed none the worse for his adventure." The watercolor illustrating this scene is hilarious—sober Tim rowing up to poor Ginger's head amidst sea gulls perched and plummeting.

Tim's parents show their concern in true Ardizzone style. His compact little mum, gazing Indian-fashion out to sea, says, "I do wish those boys would come home," and his dad murmurs, "Don't worry, my dear." Of course, the boys come bravely through, despite some very narrow, very ludicrous squeaks, and Ginger has the last and most satisfying "Poof!"

For Tim devotees, the opening lines of the very first story ("Little Tim lived in a house by the sea. He wanted very much to be a sailor") were a droll Ishmael-like call to adventure that gave great promise of wonderful things to come. That promise was fulfilled in some of the saltiest and most satisfying picture books created during the last generation. In his dad's own words, Tim "will come to no harm."

[*1966*]

It was Ginger. He was in a terrible plight.
By standing on the tips of his toes, he could
only just keep his head above the sea.

However, he was soon on board and seemed none the worse for his adventure.

Tim was tired after his long row, so he

Margaret Wise Brown
and Jean Charlot

Not long ago, as I was sorting through a pile of books that belonged to me as a child, I picked up one of my favorites and something extraordinary occurred. By just holding the book in my hands, I was able to relive the delicious first experience of reading it. The musty yellow smell of the pages brought back the summertime and the lazy days when I sat on the hot stone steps in front of my house, absorbed in the lives of the Prince and the Pauper—the streets quiet except for the singsong of the old-clothes man making his way from back yard to back yard: "Buy old clothes! Buy old clothes!" *The Prince and the Pauper* and the singsong of the old-clothes man are forever one in my memory. And the illustrations in the book are so much a part of the story that I can't remember one without the other.

This book was a miracle to me when I was a child. Now, as a working illustrator, I realize how hard it is to bring about one of these "miracles" of bookmaking. Now I know that it was a combination of things that made *The Prince and the Pauper* such an intense experience: the story, the size of the type, the illustrations, the weight and shape of the book, the binding, the shiny colored picture on the cover, the very smell of the pages.

A more recent book that has achieved this miracle is Margaret Wise Brown's *Two Little Trains*. The story is a little masterpiece of understatement. Jean Charlot is completely in tune with the story. His pictures do not merely enhance the look of the book. They live with the words in sweet harmony. They go off into playful elaborations and amplifications of the text. His choice of colors is a breathing into life of the very color of Miss Brown's words. The poignancy and drama of the journey to the West are felt by Charlot, as in:

> *Look down, look down*
> *Below the bridge,*
> *At the deep dark river*
> *Going West*

where his picture of the black waters is filled with an eerie sequence of fishes all devouring one another.

The story reveals so much more than it actually says. It is a perilous journey to the West, with rain and snow and dust storm. The two little trains chug-a-chug their way up the steep mountains that come beyond the plain, and a Charlot mountain goat arches its back in terror at the sight of them.

What I love most is the humor with which Charlot draws his sturdy little children completely undaunted by the severities of the trip. It rains and out come the umbrellas and wrap-around blankets. No fear is written on the children's faces. They sleep in undisturbed innocence under the fat half-moon while the trains hurry on. On reaching the edge of the West, the children promptly climb out of their clothes and jump into the ocean, which is big and which is blue.

I relish, too, the bobbing heads of the cattle and geese aboard the two little trains. The marvelous black-and-white snow scene, with the cattle ducking their heads down, so that only their horns show, and the passive geese with snow dripping from their bills, is perhaps my favorite. Yet, for all that, I have no favorite in the whole book. No picture could be separated from its text; they are made for each other.

The strong square look of the book is just right, and the firm black type couldn't be better. There is nothing "prissy" about this book. How easy it would have been to misunderstand Miss Brown's intentions and to make it a "cute" book! It is a rugged saga of our expanding country on one level and, for me, a very personal experience on the other. I heartily recommend it to anyone interested in the little miracles of bookmaking.

[1955]

Erik Blegvad

Erik Blegvad's illustrations perform a subtle magic for *The Dirty Old Man*, a narrative poem *(circa 1877)* by William Allingham that celebrates a worthy, if grimy, eighteenth-century gentleman named Nathaniel Bentley—better known as Dirty Dick—who for many years kept a large and motley hardware store in Leadenhall Street, London. The verses, which in Allingham's words "accord with the accounts respecting [Mr. Bentley] and his house," chronicle the fatal decline of Dirty Dick for a cause typically Victorian: despair over a lost love. Though charmingly detailed, they are routine and have "sprouted with mildewy grass," like the dirty old man's windowsills:

Full forty years since, turned the key in that door.
'Tis a room deaf and dumb 'mid the city's uproar.
The guests, for whose joyance that table was spread,
* May now enter as ghosts, for they're every one dead.*

Erik Blegvad demonstrates the genuine illustrator's sensitivity to his text. That he is in complete sympathy with *The Dirty Old Man*, yet critically alive to its weaknesses, is made clear by the manner in which he has chosen to interpret it. He explores the character beneath the shabby façade of Dirty Dick and his moldering house, and with great dexterity of pen and brush brings to life a poignant, dignified old man living in what obviously was once a resplendent and noble mansion. The portrait so superficially limned in the poem takes on in the pictures a finer dimension, but one which does not contradict William Allingham's verses.

And the drawings per se are superb. Densely textured, brimming with esoteric detail, they yet manage to convey a lightness of touch, a quality of line and color, that is suitably English. The grim, romantic reason for Dirty Dick's descent into uncleanliness (the death of his sweetheart on the eve of a momentous dinner) is mitigated by the pleasure one takes in the artist's successive studies of the ill-fated dining room, from its tastefully upholstered, oak-paneled splendor through its forty-year deterioration into a musty, cobwebbed, moonlit rat's nest.

Blegvad's pictures contribute so much to the poem, lovingly delineating, refining, and enlarging it, that gladly "Yet give we a thought free of scoffing or ban / To that Dirty Old House and that Dirty Old Man."

[*1966*]

Lou Myers

No doubt this book will be considered raucous (it is), its pictures dismissed as comic-book art (true), and its language accused of being a bit over the heads of children of picture-book age (maybe). These "flaws," however, are not what I find wrong with *Tutti-Frutti*. It tries too hard and takes too long, but I enjoy its rough, lively spirit and I think many children will relish it.

Tutti-Frutti is a very funny picture book that thumbs its nose at the stuffy, goody-goody attitudes that, year after year, continue to dominate books for the young. It offers a loud, refreshing Bronx cheer. It is an honest book and Lou Myers has a strong imagination that makes the most of some zany situations. Yes, his pictures are comic-book art, the best kind: concise, fresh, madly animated. It is too bad that this style of drawing is so often contemptuously dismissed as unsuitable in books for children. It is, after all, only a *style*, one that can be as expressive as any other in the hands of a real artist, such as Lou Myers. More important, we should allow a place for picture books like *Tutti-Frutti*. It is a noisy book that takes account of our very noisy world.

[*1967*]

Tomi Ungerer
Harriet Pincus
Edward Ardizzone
Harve and
Margot Zemach

Tomi Ungerer has never failed the picture book. Unlike the well-meaning but uninspired illustrators who grapple with, misuse, and occasionally deface this form, Ungerer instinctively understands the poetry and technical demands inherent in it. *Moon Man*, in its originality of conception, individual statement, and beauty of execution, is easily one of the best picture books in recent years. It is pertinent, contemporary, coolly acid in tone, and altogether beguiling. Of course, since it's by Ungerer, it is also very funny.

Ungerer's style is at once dramatically simple and overflowing in comic overtone. His ideas are condensed, everything superfluous strained out, and the result is a grand and forceful marriage of language and art. Some adults look at his work, then rush to drag out the bromide that explains how easy it is to make a picture book: "Just a handful of sentences and a lot of blazing pictures." These critics fail to see that a successful picture book is a visual poem. Ungerer has the kind of eye that is needed to recognize the potential in an abbreviated, bareboned text; like the exceptional poet who can gracefully meet the demands of terza rima or write a good sonnet, he knows how to create the satisfying balance of language and illustration that marks a picture book worthy of the name. *Moon Man* can stand as a model of how it all works.

Ungerer's pictures for this book *are* blazingly beautiful, but they also keep time, never outpace, and always enlarge on his concise "handful of sentences." He is a master of design, a great draftsman, a colorist par excellence, and he is further endowed with a wickedly accurate eye for caricature. The Strangelove types who proliferate in the pages of *Moon Man* are delightfully bizarre, even to the wild-eyed, demented dog on page 14. In the midst of this madness, plump, bluish-white Moon Man, though no beauty, provokes just enough sympathy. His droll escape from the prison cell is Ungerer at his best. The book is full of sly details that slip easily into the grand scheme without once roughing up the smooth surface. They are details that might, without careful inspection, go unnoticed. But we can trust the children to notice.

Ungerer seems to prefer a certain detachment from his material. His personal statement is intellectual rather than emotional, whereas Harriet Pincus's interpretation of Carl Sandburg's *The Wedding Procession of the Rag Doll and the Broom Handle and Who Was in It* is a purely emotional one. She is not, as yet, capable of Ungerer's dazzling craft and technical skill, and her details tend at times to be careless and not freshly observed. But (putting aside the fact that this is her first book) Miss Pincus's interest in graphics is something different from Ungerer's. Design, color, and details are subservient to her main goal—endowing her text with the intensity of her private vision—and Miss Pincus has more than sufficient skill to fulfill that. It is a lovely vision and it belongs exclusively to Harriet Pincus. Her book is like a glimpse into the inner workings of her heart.

I would not have imagined the Sandburg story capable of bearing the weight of such a personal interpretation, but it turns out to be an excellent picturebook text. It is terrifying, though, to think how badly it might have been illustrated—impossibly "cute" or deadly cheerful. The marvel of Harriet Pincus's talent lies in her ability to interpret Sandburg in a manner that gives an appropriate new dimension to his story and at the same time creates a world that belongs only to Pincus.

It is difficult to describe her particular world. Its dreamlike quality is extremely compelling, and I find myself, when looking at her pictures, almost recalling something of my own childhood. Miss Pincus's images have a heartbreaking truthfulness. Although there is nothing sad about them, she manages to convey, besides buoyancy and vigor, an undefined poignancy that more than anything else catches the vulnerability of childhood. *The Wedding Procession of the Rag Doll* is imbued with Harriet Pincus's fine sensibility and insight. It is an example of the flexibility, depth, and originality a new artist can bring to the picture book, a form that nowadays is so often merely commercial, worn out, and vulgar.

Edward Ardizzone's work, though appreciated by many, is too often taken for granted. *The Dragon*, with story by Archibald Marshall, is a charming example of the various and unique abilities of this artist, who is possibly the best contemporary example of the quintessential illustrator. He works wonders in *The Dragon*, and these whirlwind-rendered watercolors—

which look careless to the dull-minded—are some of his finest. Mr. Marshall's story sidesteps the pedestrian dragon-slayer-and-princess routine with some funny turns of events; Ardizzone caps these moments and rounds out the story with some witty twists of his own. As is usual for him, he performs like a sympathetic pianist who supports and shows to best advantage the singer he is accompanying.

Ardizzone's fluid style makes no concessions to the young, but only a pedantic child could fret over the few pictorial inconsistencies. Most children will be busy with the lugubrious, empty-headed dragon as he plods his way through the kingdom, matter-of-factly snatching victims and blowing smoke and fire with the regularity of a steam engine.

Two of the last pictures in the book are fine examples of Ardizzone's eye for the telling moment. One depicts the dragon, in the far background, placidly devouring the bald, middle-aged Prince so detested by the Princess; in the foreground—besides the King, the Princess, and her young lover, and unimportant to the action—sits a humble page, devouring his less gory meal of bread and wine. The juxtaposition of dragon and page and the unconcern of all involved are typical Ardizzone touches. The other picture portrays the dragon's death with grandeur and monumentality. In the act of dying, the dragon gains a dignity never revealed before. It is a startling final flourish.

Ardizzone's design—from page to page and within each page—is functional but, unlike Ungerer's, contributes little dramatically to (though it never detracts from) the story. Margot Zemach expertly uses design to her own ends in *Too Much Nose*. She achieves rhythm and pacing reminiscent of Chaplin's. Her sense of comedy also has much in common with his, and she never misses a chance to make us laugh. She

chooses her moment—brings your eye to it on the page
—with the unerring deftness of a master humorist.

Harve Zemach's deadpan, pseudo-serious story is an
ideal vehicle for Mrs. Zemach's talents. He follows
the traditional form of the fairy tale, tongue firmly in
cheek and eye fixed on his inventive wife, leaving her
plenty of room to carry on in her typically unpredictable manner. Who but Margot Zemach would
imagine the mysterious Someone, a sort of genie who
comes out of a battered magic horn, as a blowzy,
bellicose old harridan? Great! Her sad-eyed, poker-
faced characters move through their absurd silent-
movie pantomimes with polished dexterity. Her people
don't merely fall down; they perform an intricate
aerial ballet before they touch ground, and their sober
faces reveal nothing of this incredible hidden talent.
As for the nitwit queen sulkily playing solitaire while
her immense nose gets in the way—only Zemach
could have conjured her up.

There are too many funny touches in *Too Much
Nose* to take account of here. It is enough to say that
Margot Zemach's work—her superlative drawing, her
inexhaustibly original humor, her shrewd use of
design—greatly enlivens the picture-book scene. She
understands what a picture book is and can be, and
treats the form with the passion and artistry that are
shamefully lacking in too many picture books published today.

[*1967*]

Arthur Yorinks
and Richard Egielski

Sid and Sol is a wonder—a picture book that
heralds a hopeful, healthy flicker of life in what is becoming a creatively exhausted genre. The magic rests
in the seamless bond of Arthur Yorinks and Richard
Egielski's deft and exciting collaboration.

Sol is a giant. "Tremendous. He was bigger than a
thousand midgets on each other's shoulders. He was
bigger than the tallest building. He was BIG." (These
short, spiky opening sentences delight me. They have,
to my ear, the sharp staccato sound of movie language,
as though the book were being introduced by no less a
star than James Cagney.) Sol delights in his size and
strength. "He liked to tremble the world." And the
world, desperate, advertises for a giant-killer. After a
long wait, Sid comes along. (Sid *is* James Cagney—
see him soft-shoe his way in and out of the world
leaders' office.) "Sid, the whole world wishes you good
luck," the moguls tell him, but Mr. Yorinks, never
the false optimist, wryly adds, "The world thought the
worst."

That very day, however, Sol gets his comeuppance
in a sly, original fashion—which I won't spoil for the
reader. Enough to say that the results are bizarre and

immensely funny. Like the hectic hodgepodge mountain Sol wildly piles up—composed, shockingly, of some of the world's most sacred icons (Mount Rushmore and the Eiffel Tower, for example)—the book, too, is a hodgepodge of variations on the runt/giant theme, from David and Goliath to Jack the Giant Killer, all seen through the nostalgic glow of a 1940s movie.

Curiously, the book is reminiscent of old, good things. But the childhood feelings it evokes, and the nostalgia for a past time and place, could not have been experienced firsthand by the two young artists who created this marvelous book; they are of another generation.

The surprise in *Sid and Sol* is that both Arthur Yorinks's daring text and Richard Egielski's innovative pictures convey the very essence of another time in American books and film. It is not the heavy-handed, commercial, star-struck nostalgia for the thirties and forties that currently threatens to inundate us, but rather the clear-eyed, unsentimental view of two young and gifted artists.

Mr. Yorinks has the cool audacity to mix absolute nonsense with cockeyed fact. Almost as an aside, the book offers an upside-down *National Geographic* explanation of the creation of the Grand Canyon. This is inspired, stand-up-comic stuff and gorgeous writing. Mr. Yorinks is refreshingly free with both sentence structure and language—i.e., "with a shivery timber" —but there is no self-indulgence at work here. The cunning dryness and terse emphasis of the text are shrewdly calculated. And the pictures do the fleshing out. That's what picture books are all about.

Richard Egielski catches the preposterousness of Mr. Yorinks's nimble text in a series of ravishing black-and-white stills—movie stills that not only mirror the text but amplify and add weight in just the right places. Page by page, the illustrator matches the daring of the writer. And Mr. Egielski's black-and-white tonalities have a loveliness and sheer sensuality I've seen nowhere before. They render perfectly the silver-screen image. Aside from his dazzling polish, he is just plain brave. He can even turn one double spread sideways and it comes off. When Sol's laughter "trembles" the world, the whole spread shivers and shakes.

Mr. Egielski is clever enough to break the uniformity of his frames, allowing for mischievous and sometimes disturbing contours. His solution for the first double-page spread illustrating Sol's gigantism—to frame one of the giant's feet on each side of the spread—is a triumph. And the picture of Sol's demise is one of the most original double spreads I've ever seen.

The story ends happily, sort of. But the true miracle is how, together, these two artists tell their tale without ever telegraphing what's about to happen—or, for that matter, even trying to convince us of that traditional, tacked-on happy ending. Despite the words about Sid's good fortune and the picture of him, cocktail in hand, on his Taj Mahalian estate, our hero seems definitely lonely and disenchanted with the world he has conquered.

The picture book, as I can attest, is a fiendishly difficult form. There is no margin for error; one small slip and the book collapses. *Sid and Sol* is a brand-new venture for both its young artists, and it works. Welcome, Arthur Yorinks and Richard Egielski!

[*1978*]

Two

Caldecott Medal
Acceptance

This talk will be an attempt to answer a question. It is one that is frequently put to me, and it goes something like this: Where did you ever get such a crazy, scary idea for a book? Of course the question refers to *Where the Wild Things Are*. My on-the-spot answer always amounts to an evasive "Out of my head." And that usually provokes a curious and sympathetic stare at my unfortunate head, as though—à la Dr. Jekyll—I were about to prove my point by sprouting horns and a neat row of pointy fangs.

It is an incredibly difficult question. But if I turn to the work of Randolph Caldecott and define the single element that, in my opinion, most accounts for his greatness, then I think I can begin to answer it. Besides, this gives me an excuse to talk about some of the qualities I most enjoy in the work of one of my favorite teachers.

I can't think of Caldecott without thinking of music and dance. *The Three Jovial Huntsmen* beautifully demonstrates his affinity for musical language. It is a

[*This acceptance speech was given on June 30, 1964, at the meeting of the American Library Association in St. Louis, Missouri*]

songbook animated by a natural, easy, contrapuntal play between words and pictures. The action is paced to the beat of a perky march, a comic fugue, and an English country dance—I can hear the music as I turn the pages.

I am infatuated with the musical accompaniment Caldecott provides in his books, for I have reached for that very quality in my own. In fact, music is essential to my work. I feel an intense sympathy between the shape of a musical phrase and that of a drawn line. Sketching to music is a marvelous stimulant to my imagination, and often a piece of music will give me the needed clue to the look and color of a picture. It is exciting to search for just the right color on paper that Wagner found in a musical phrase to conjure up a magic forest.

No one in a Caldecott book ever stands still. If the characters are not dancing, they are itching to dance. They never walk; they skip. Almost the first we see of The Great Panjandrum Himself is his foot, and its attitude makes us suspect that the rest of his hidden self is dancing a jig. I remember my own delight in choreographing dances for picture-book characters; my favorite is a bouncy ballet some Ruth Krauss children danced to a Haydn serenade. I think Caldecott would have been sympathetic to such extravagances, for he was endowed with a fabulous sense of lively animation, a quality he shares with my other favorite illustrators: Boutet de Monvel, Wilhelm Busch, Hans Fischer, and André François. Characters who dance and leap across the page, loudly proclaiming their personal independence of the paper—this is perhaps the most charming feature of a Caldecott picture book. Think of his three clowning huntsmen, red in the face, tripping, sagging, blowing frantically on their horns, receding hilariously into the distance and then gallop-

RANDOLPH CALDECOTT / *The Three Jovial Huntsmen*

And the Dish ran away with the Spoon.

ing full-blast back at you. It has the vivacity of a silent movie, and the huntsmen are three perfect Charlie Chaplins.

One can forever delight in the liveliness and physical ease of Caldecott's picture books, in his ingenious and playful elaborations on a given text. But so far as I am concerned, these enviable qualities only begin to explain Caldecott's supremacy. For me, his greatness lies in the truthfulness of his vision of life. There is no emasculation of truth in his world. It is a green, vigorous world rendered faithfully and honestly in shades of dark and light, a world where the tragic and the joyful coexist, the one coloring the other. It encompasses three slaphappy huntsmen, as well as the ironic death of a mad, misunderstood dog; it allows for country lads and lasses flirting and dancing round the Maypole, as well as Baby Bunting's startled realization that her rabbit skin came from a creature that was once alive.

My favorite example of Caldecott's fearless honesty is the final page of *Hey Diddle Diddle*. After we read "And the Dish ran away with the Spoon," accompanied by a drawing of the happy couple, there is the shock of turning the page and finding a picture of the dish broken into ten pieces—obviously dead—and the spoon being hustled away by her angry parents, a fork and a knife. There are no words that suggest such an end to the adventure; it is a purely Caldecottian invention. Apparently, he could not resist enlarging the dimensions of this jaunty nursery rhyme by adding a last sorrowful touch.

Caldecott never tells half-truths about life, and his honest vision, expressed with such conviction, is one that children recognize as true to their own lives.

Truthfulness to life—both fantasy life and factual life—is the basis of all great art. This is the beginning of my answer to the question: Where did you get such a crazy, scary idea for a book? I believe I can try to answer it now if it is rephrased as follows: What is your vision of the truth, and what has it to do with children?

During my early teens I spent hundreds of hours sitting at my window, sketching neighborhood children at play. I sketched and listened, and those notebooks became the fertile field of my work later on. There is not a book I have written or a picture I have drawn that does not, in some way, owe them its existence. Last fall, soon after finishing *Where the Wild Things Are*, I sat on the front porch of my parents' house in Brooklyn and witnessed a scene that could have been a page from one of those early notebooks. I might have titled it "Arnold the Monster."

Arnold was a tubby, pleasant-faced little boy who could instantly turn himself into a howling, groaning, hunched horror—a composite of Frankenstein's monster, the Werewolf, and Godzilla. His willing victims were four giggling little girls, whom he chased frantically around parked automobiles and up and down front steps. The girls would flee, hiccuping and shrieking, "Oh, help! Save me! The monster will eat me!" And Arnold would lumber after them, rolling his eyes and bellowing. The noise was ear-splitting, the proceedings were fascinating.

At one point, carried away by his frenzy, Arnold broke an unwritten rule of such games. He actually caught one of his victims. She was furious. "You're not supposed to catch me, dope," she said, and smacked Arnold. He meekly apologized, and a moment later this same little girl dashed away screaming the game song: "Oh, help! Save me!" etc. The children became hot and mussed-looking. They had the glittery look of primitive creatures going through a ritual dance.

The game ended in a collapse of exhaustion. Arnold dragged himself away, and the girls went off with a look of sweet peace on their faces. A mysterious inner battle had been played out, and their minds and bodies were at rest, for the moment.

I have watched children play many variations of this game. They are the necessary games children must conjure up to combat an awful fact of childhood: the fact of their vulnerability to fear, anger, hate, frustration—all the emotions that are an ordinary part of their lives and that they can perceive only as ungovernable and dangerous forces. To master these forces, children turn to fantasy: that imagined world where disturbing emotional situations are solved to their satisfaction. Through fantasy, Max, the hero of my book, discharges his anger against his mother, and returns to the real world sleepy, hungry, and at peace with himself.

Certainly we want to protect our children from new and painful experiences that are beyond their emotional comprehension and that intensify anxiety; and to a point we can prevent premature exposure to such experiences. That is obvious. But what is just as obvious—and what is too often overlooked—is the fact that from their earliest years children live on familiar terms with disrupting emotions, that fear and anxiety are an intrinsic part of their everyday lives, that they continually cope with frustration as best they can. And it is through fantasy that children achieve catharsis. It is the best means they have for taming Wild Things.

It is my involvement with this inescapable fact of childhood—the awful vulnerability of children and their struggle to make themselves King of All Wild Things—that gives my work whatever truth and passion it may have.

Max is my bravest and therefore my dearest creation. Like all children, he believes in a flexible world of fantasy and reality, a world where a child can skip from one to the other and back again in the sure belief that both really exist. Another quality that makes him especially lovable to me is the directness of his approach. Max doesn't shilly-shally about. He gets to the heart of the matter with the speed of a superjet, a personality trait that is happily suited to the necessary visual simplicity of a picture book.

Max has appeared in my other books under different names: Kenny, Martin, and Rosie. They all have the same need to master the uncontrollable and frightening aspects of their lives, and they all turn to fantasy to accomplish this. Kenny struggles with confusion; Rosie, with boredom and a sense of personal inadequacy; and Martin, with frustration.

On the whole, they are a serious lot. Someone once criticized me for representing children as little old people worrying away their childhood. I do not deny that a somber element colors my vision of childhood, but I reject the implication that this is not a true vision. It seems a distortion, rather, to pretend to a child that his life is a never-ending ring-around-the-rosie. Childhood *is* a difficult time. We know it is a marvelous time as well—perhaps even the best time of all. Obviously all children's games are not therapeutic attempts to exorcise fear; often they are just for fun.

Max, too, is having fun, and not by playing hide-and-seek with Sigmund Freud. He is delighted at having conjured up his horrific beasts, and their willingness to be ordered about by an aggressive miniature king is, for Max, his wildest dream come true. My experience suggests that the adults who are troubled by the scariness of his fantasy forget that my hero is having the time of his life and that he controls the situation with breezy aplomb. Children do watch Max. They pick up his confidence and sail through the adventure, deriving, I sincerely hope, as much fun as he does. These are the children who send me their own drawings of Wild Things: monstrous, hair-raising visions; dream creatures, befanged and beclawed, towering King Kong–like over jungle islands. They make my Wild Things look like cuddly fuzzballs.

The realities of childhood put to shame the half-true notions in some children's books. These offer a gilded world unshadowed by the least suggestion of conflict or pain, a world manufactured by those who cannot—or don't care to—remember the truth of their own childhood. Their expurgated vision has no relation to the way real children live.

I suppose these books have some purpose—they don't frighten adults, those adults who cling to the great nineteenth-century fantasy that paints childhood as an eternally innocent paradise. These so-called children's books are published under false colors, for they serve only to indulge grownups. They are passed from adult to adult, for they could only be loved by adults who have a false and sentimental recollection of childhood. My own guess is that they bore the eyeteeth out of children.

The popularity of such books is proof of endless pussyfooting about the grim aspects of child life, pussyfooting that attempts to justify itself by reminding us that we must not frighten our children. Of course we must avoid frightening children, if by that we mean protecting them from experiences beyond their emotional capabilities; but I doubt that this is what most people mean when they say "We must not frighten our children." The need for evasive books is the most obvious indication of the common wish to protect children from their everyday fears and anxieties, a hopeless wish that denies the child's endless battle with disturbing emotions.

Ursula Nordstrom has been a lifelong friend. I say "lifelong" because the best part of my life began when I was able to put my talents to use, and she was there to creatively guide me. She earned new respect from me when she confessed her squeamishness on seeing the first pictures for *Where the Wild Things Are*. This admission of misgivings and her realization that she was reacting in stereotyped adult fashion was a confession of utmost truth, and only she could have made it. This is how she put it recently: "And so we remembered once again, as so many times in the past, that the children are new and we are not." Her support and unflagging enthusiasm helped bring the book to a happy conclusion.

And I will not easily forget the pale face of Dorothy Hagen, art director, her sad, suicidal look at the prospect of examining yet another sheet of color proofs. I owe her much.

With *Where the Wild Things Are* I feel that I am at the end of a long apprenticeship. By that I mean all my previous work now seems to have been an elaborate preparation for it. I believe it is an immense step forward for me, a critical stage in my work, and your awarding this book the Caldecott Medal gives me further incentive to continue that work. For that, I am especially grateful.

Where the Wild Things Are was not meant to please everybody—only children. A letter from a seven-year-old boy encourages me to think that I have reached children as I had hoped. He wrote: "How much does it cost to get to where the wild things are? If it is not expensive my sister and I want to spend the summer there. Please answer soon." I did not answer that question, for I have no doubt that sooner or later they will find their way, free of charge.

[*1964*]

Balsa Wood
and Fairy Tales

In a recent issue of *The New York Times*, a special advertising section provided interesting reading. A company that manufactures children's toys, more specifically model kits, had this to say while extolling the virtues of its products:

In former times, the making of a model airplane required real talent—almost the ability of a sculptor—to achieve even passable results. Many a young man developed a what's-the-use attitude; many a young aspirant came to feel the pangs of frustration. Today, the builder knows he can be successful if he applies himself diligently, if he is patient and careful.

These depressing words provoked happy memories of childhood: my brother and I constructing model airplanes, applying ourselves diligently, with patience and care; painstakingly forming the delicate balsa wood into wing shapes; holding our breath while covering these fragile shapes with too-thin pink tissue paper. The risks were high, and more often than not the results were calamitous. But I know without any doubt that the risks made it all worthwhile. The frustration, the anger and confusion were all part of the fun. We were not Brooklyn Leonardos; and though perfection was the goal, I believe we accepted with a fair amount of grace our artistic shortcomings and settled more or less happily for an airplane whose propeller whirled properly and whose delicate frame smashed thrillingly against the kitchen wall.

I don't think I'm stretching the point when I suggest that this "let's-make-the-world-a-happy-easy-frustrationless-place-for-the-kids" attitude is often propounded in children's literature today. There are, however, many enlightened people in the field who think the creative artist has greater scope of subject matter than ever before. But, even so, I believe there exists a quiet but highly effective adult censorship of subjects that are supposedly too frightening, or morbid, or not optimistic enough, for boys and girls.

This should be of little importance to the creative artist whose prime concern is exploring the riches of his own remembered childhood and presenting them transmuted into artistic form for children. The artist can have—and should have—no hope of satisfying all children, just as the novelist cannot aim to please all readers. There is room, however, in the world of adult books for all kinds of writing and all manner of tastes. It seems to me that just the opposite exists in children's literature. There is a stereotype for children's books that hinders the oddball or "different" kind of book.

Clearly the brothers Grimm and Mr. H. C. Andersen never bothered their heads about providing so-called healthy or suitable literature for children. How fortunate for us they were only interested in telling a good story! And they are stories charged with originality and a tremendous understanding of the fascinating tangle of life—written with style and taste,

offering a real world distilled into fantasy, which up-
sets the delicate insides of children less than it does the
adults'.

Ursula Nordstrom, children's book editor at Harper
and Row, said it best:

It is always the adults we have to contend with—most
children under the age of ten will react creatively to the
best work of a truly creative person. But too often adults
sift their reactions to creative picture books through their
own adult experiences. And as an editor who stands between the creative artist and the creative child I am constantly terrified that I will react as a dull adult. But at least
I must try to remember it every minute!

[1964]

Fantasy Sketches

This is a sampling from a large collection of fantasy pages that I drew over five years or so, roughly 1952 to 1957. In one way or another, all such drawings of this period hint at themes that later were developed in my books for children. In fact, they touch *all* the obsessions and ideas that eventually bore fruit in what I consider my best and most personal work.

After 1957, I abandoned this particular form altogether. It had been a source of gratification, but I suspect that at some point I began consciously to manipulate my unconscious, and it was then that I was compelled to quit. Perhaps in their short time, these drawings had served their full purpose, though I could never define what their purpose was. I could only call them by vague and various names: fantasy sketches, stream-of-consciousness doodles, dream pictures, and, probably most apt, homework drawings. They came at a time when I apparently needed to exercise my imagination, to work my themes onto paper.

[*Preface to* Maurice Sendak: Fantasy Sketches, *published by the Rosenbach Museum and Library, Philadelphia*]

MAURICE SENDAK / *A fantasy sketched to Deems Taylor's*
Through the Looking Glass

Music, which accompanied the creation of these pages, is the catalyst that brought them to life. They were never intended, however, to be specific illustrations for musical compositions. Music helped unravel my imaginary scenes; it pressed the button, turned the key, kept my pen moving across the paper. My homework consisted of letting whatever came into my mind come out on the paper, and my only conscious intention was to complete a whole "story" on one page, to compose the whole sheet, beginning and ending, if possible, with the music itself. Sometimes I worked to a recording of a symphony, my eye allowing just so much space on the page for each movement. More often I worked to chamber music, and best were the short piano pieces that practically guaranteed a page finished safely.

Some of these pages are stories in the conventional sense. More are fantastic meanderings that seem to roam carelessly through the unconscious. Others are attempts to choreograph the music, a kind of pen-and-ink ballet. They all are my fantasy attempts to "compose songs," to set music to pictures—to act out indirectly my frustrated ambition to be a composer.

Perhaps all, perhaps none of these reasons is the explanation for the existence of these until now unpublished drawings. My affection for them despite their rough composition and clumsy execution is indicative of their special and private importance to me. They are the only homework to which I energetically applied myself, the only school that ever taught me anything.

[*1970*]

Some of My Pictures

Affection and a suitably prejudiced view of my own work bind these nineteen pictures together. They are some of the pictures I like best, selected from eight of the seventy books I have illustrated over the past twenty years.

The choices, I thought, would be easy to make; I know which of my pictures I prefer. But I found that many of my favorite illustrations of the fifties are irrevocably bound to their texts. Separated from the words they are meant to accompany, they pale. Others from this period that could successfully stand on their own no longer satisfy me. In the end, I eliminated all my books published in the fifties, some thirty-five of them.

It was hard passing up these books, but for the purposes of this portfolio I was much more successful in the following decade. The 1860s, the great years of the English illustrators from whom so much of my work is derived, are familiarly known as "the sixties" to admirers of Victorian book illustration. What good

[*Preface to* Pictures by Maurice Sendak, *a portfolio published by Harper and Row*]

luck, for an artist who is happily haunted by this particular past, to have my own private sixties.

The influence of Victorian artists such as George Pinwell and Arthur Hughes, to name just two, is evident in the pictures for *Higglety Pigglety Pop!* (1967), *Zlateh the Goat* (1966), and *A Kiss for Little Bear* (1968). And I've learned from other English artists as well. Randolph Caldecott gave me my first demonstration of the subtle uses of rhythm and structure in a picture book. (*Hector Protector and As I Went Over the Water* of 1965, represented here by one illustration, is an intentionally contrived homage to this beloved teacher.) For other fine points in picture-book making, I have studied the work of Beatrix Potter and William Nicholson. Nicholson's *The Pirate Twins* certainly influenced *Where the Wild Things Are.*

A retrospective of my English obsession can be found in *Lullabies and Night Songs* (1965). The illustrations for this book, which skip from Rowlandson to Cruikshank to Caldecott and even to Blake, are a noisy pastiche of styles, though I believe they still resonate with my own particular sound. The three offered here are definitely favorites, despite their grabby eclecticism.

The earliest pictures in this portfolio are from *Mr. Rabbit and the Lovely Present* (1962), as far as I am aware the only book I've done that reveals my admiration for Winslow Homer.

Where the Wild Things Are (1963), a favorite child, is represented by four illustrations. Besides owing much to Caldecott and Nicholson, this book must acknowledge stylistic kinship to French and German book illustration of the nineteenth century. I was thirty-five when I did *Wild Things*, still looking to Europe and back a hundred years for creative roots. My immediate past, everything I grew up with, though tenderly treasured in memory, was useless to me an artist; or so I apparently believed.

The unconscious, thank heavens, goes its own way, ignoring the mumbo-jumbo sophistries of the head up front. *Wild Things*, despite its European credentials, is the first book of mine in which I see a glimmer of interest in confronting and exploiting a kind of art I had known all my life. This is said with a good deal of hindsight and with the accomplishment of *In the Night Kitchen* (1970) behind me. That book is influenced not by an artistic mode of the past that I consider superior but by art that was available and potent to a child growing up in America in the thirties and forties. *Night Kitchen* and, to a lesser degree, *Wild Things* reflect a popular American art both crass and oddly surrealistic, an art that encompasses the Empire State Building, syncopated Disney cartoons, and aluminum-clad comic-book heroes, an Art Moderne that was most sensuously catalogued in the movies. What Caldecott is to *Hector Protector*, the monster movie is to *Wild Things*. What the Victorian illustrators are to *Higglety Pigglety Pop!*, Busby Berkeley and Mickey Mouse are to *Night Kitchen*. This is oversimplification, of course, but the truth lies somewhere inside.

About two and a half years after the publication of *Where the Wild Things Are*, I finally became conscious of my reviving interest in the art I had experienced and loved as a child. The trigger was an exhibit of pages from *Little Nemo in Slumberland*, Winsor McCay's epic comic strip. Before the exhibit I had apparently underestimated this popular American artist's genius for graphic fantasy. It now sent me scooting back with new eyes to the popular art of my own childhood.

This recognition of personal roots is in no way

meant as a triumphant revelation or as reverse snobbism, a put-down of my earlier, more "refined" influences. What I have learned from English as well as French and German artists will, if I have my wish, become more absorbed into my creative psyche, blending and living peaceably with my own slice of the past. But, of course, all this happens on its own or it doesn't happen at all.

[*1971*]

Hans Christian Andersen
Medal Acceptance

All my life I have been fortunate enough to do the work that comes naturally and spontaneously to me: illustrating and writing books for children. Happily, an essential part of myself—my dreaming life—still lives in the potent, urgent light of childhood; in my case, an American childhood composed of strangely concocted elements. I had a conglomerate fantasy life as a child, typical of many first-generation children in America, particularly those in a land called Brooklyn, a regulated, tree-lined ghetto-land separated only by a river from the most magical of all lands, New York City—that fantastic place rarely visited but much dreamed of.

Mine was a childhood colored with memories of village life in Poland, never actually experienced but passed on to me as persuasive reality by my immigrant parents. On the one hand, I lived snugly in their Old Country world, a world far from urban society, where the laws and customs of a small Jewish village were scrupulously and lovingly obeyed. And on the other hand, I was bombarded with the in-

[*This acceptance speech was given on April 4, 1970, in Bologna, Italy*]

toxicating gush of America in that convulsed decade,
the thirties. Two emblems represent that era for me: a
photograph of my severe, bearded grandfather (I
never actually saw him), which haunts me to this day
and which, as a child, I believed to be the exact image
of God; and Mickey Mouse. These two lived side by
side in a bizarre togetherness that I accepted as
natural. For me, childhood was shtetl life transplanted,
Brooklyn colored by Old World reverberations and
Walt Disney and the occasional trip to the incredibly
windowed "uptown" that was New York–America.
All in all, what with loving parents and sister and
brother, it was a satisfying childhood. Was it American? Everybody's America is different.

And then there were the books I loved—those cheap,
pulp-papered, bad-smelling, gorgeously if vulgarly
colored comic books and storybooks, full of mystifying
magic men and women dressed in gleaming costumes
and whizzing over some great American metropolis
and into the vast unknown. Best of all, perhaps, were
the movies of my childhood. With their exotic, glossy
fantasticalness, they permanently dyed my imagination a silvery Hollywood color. Aspects of the movies
that might be rejected by an adult mind were perfectly
suited to a child devoted to making up stories and,
from an early age, putting them down on paper. The
pleasurably dreaded movie monsters, the graphically
vivid, absurdly endearing figures of Mickey Mouse
and Charlie Chaplin were the most direct influences
on me as a young artist.

As a child I felt that books were holy objects, to be
caressed, rapturously sniffed, and devotedly provided
for. I gave my life to them—I still do. I continue to do
what I did as a child: dream of books, make books,
and collect books. As I grew older and could cross that
river with ease into a New York that remained magi-

cal, my taste and interest in books became more sophisticated. On my own I discovered artists from all over the world who seemed to speak directly to me; and as a young man, trying to discover my creative self, I leaned heavily on these sympathetic friends. They were a very cultivated bunch. From the first, my great and abiding love was William Blake, my teacher in all things. And from two other Englishmen, Thomas Rowlandson and George Cruikshank, I borrowed techniques and tried to forge them into a personal language. The Frenchman Boutet de Monvel refined my eye and quickened my heart and ambition. The Germans Wilhelm Busch and Heinrich Hoffmann provided me with the basis of a style and hinted at a kind of content that developed much later in my own work. When I was sixteen I first saw the edition of *Pinocchio* illustrated by Attilio Mussino, and I know that was a turning point. My eyes were opened by the offhand virtuosity of the man, the ease with which he commanded a variety of styles, controlling them all, blending them, and still managing to keep them subservient to the tale. He taught me at one and the same time respect for finish and style as well as a certain disregard for these qualities. Style counts, I now saw, only insofar as it conveys the inner meaning of the text being illustrated.

There were other artists who taught me, who coaxed me into becoming myself—too many to bring up here. But I cannot leave unmentioned the great Swiss illustrators—Rodolphe Töpffer, Ernst Kreidolf, and Hans Fischer, all of whom influenced me significantly during my apprentice years.

My passion for making books has lately led me to a distinct vision of what I want my books to be, a vision difficult to verbalize. I am now in search of a form more purely and essentially my own. In a way I'd rather have been a composer of operas and songs, and I must turn to music to describe something of what I am after. The concentrated face of Verdi's *Falstaff* or a Hugo Wolf song—where music and words mix and blend and incredibly excite—defines my ideal. Here words and music form a magic compound, a "something else," more than music, more than words. My wish is to combine—in words and pictures, faithfully and fantastically—my weird, Old Country–New Country childhood; my obsession with shtetl life, its spirit; and the illuminating visions especially loved artists have shown me. All this, mixed and beaten and smoothed into a picture-book form that has something resembling the lush, immediate beauty of music and all its deep, unanalyzable mystery. Most of all, the mystery—that is the cherished goal.

Hans Christian Andersen described his life as a fairy tale, a pronouncement that, taken literally, might provoke a shudder or bring to mind a particular coyness that has often been detrimental to the serious work of writing and illustrating for children. But, in the metaphoric sense Andersen intended, I can say the same thing and mean it. As a small boy I pasted and clipped my bits of books together and hoped only for a life that would permit me to earn my bread by pasting and clipping more bits of books. And here I am, all grown up—at least physically—and *still* at home making books.

I want to thank you for forever linking my name with Andersen's. This great honor is the coming together of all my various worlds.

[*1970*]

A Conversation with Virginia Haviland

VIRGINIA HAVILAND: *What did a book mean to you as a child? And what kinds of books did you have?*

MAURICE SENDAK: My sister bought me my first real book, *The Prince and the Pauper*. A ritual began with that book. The first thing was to set it up on the table and stare at it for a long time. Not because I was impressed with Mark Twain; it was just such a beautiful object. Then came the smelling of it. I think the smelling of books began with *The Prince and the Pauper*, because it was printed on particularly fine paper, unlike my Disney books from the five-and-ten, which were printed on very poor paper and smelled bad. *The Prince and the Paper—Pauper—* smelled good and it also had a shiny cover, a laminated cover. I flipped over that. And it was very solid. I remember trying to bite into it, which I don't imagine is what my sister intended when she bought the book for me. But the last thing I did with the book was to read it. It was all right. But I think it started then, a love for books and bookmaking. There's so much more to a book than just the reading. I've seen children play with books, fondle books, smell books, and that's every reason why books should be lovingly produced.

What part do you think fantasy should play in a child's life?

Fantasy is all-pervasive in a child's life. I believe there's no part of our lives—our adult as well as child life—when we're not fantasizing, but we prefer to relegate fantasy to children, as though it were some tomfoolery only fit for the immature minds of the young. Children do live in fantasy and reality, in a way we no longer remember. They have a cool sense of the logic of illogic, and they shift very easily from one sphere to another. Fantasy is the core of all writing for children, as I think it is for the writing of any book, for any creative act, perhaps for the act of living. But these fantasies have to be given physical form, so you build a house around them, and the house is what you call a story, and the painting of the house is the bookmaking. But essentially it's a dream, or a fantasy.

Many persons right now are asking what inspired you to produce this new book, In the Night Kitchen.

There are a few clues. When I was a child, there was an advertisement which I remember too clearly. It was for the Sunshine Bakers. And the advertisement read "We Bake While You Sleep!" It seemed to me the most sadistic thing in the world, because all I wanted to do was stay up and watch. And it seemed so absurdly cruel and arbitrary for them to do it while I slept. And also for them to think I would think that was terrific. I remember I used to save the coupons showing the three fat little Sunshine bakers going off to this yummy place, wherever it was, to have their fun, while I had to go to bed. This book is a vendetta, a way to get back at them and say that now I'm old enough to stay up late and see what's going on in the Night Kitchen. Another clue is a rather odd fantasy of mine when I was a child. I lived in Brooklyn, and traveling to Manhattan was a big deal, even though it was so close. I couldn't go by myself, and had to depend on my older sister. She took us—my brother and me—to Radio City Music Hall, or the Roxy, or some such place. Now, the point of going to New York was that you *ate* in New York. Somehow, to me, New York signified eating—eating in a fashionable, elegant, mysterious place like Longchamps. You got dressed up, and you went uptown, and it was night when you got there, and there were lots of windows blinking, and you went straight to a place to eat. It was one of the most exciting treats of my childhood. Cross the bridge, and see the city approaching, and get there, and have your dinner, and then go to a movie, and come home. So *In the Night Kitchen* is a kind of homage to New York City, the city I loved so much and still love. It also pays homage to works of art— such as they were—that affected me powerfully. I did not get to museums, I did not see art books. *Fantasia* was *the* artistic experience of my childhood, and that was a mixed blessing. But mainly there were comic books and there was Walt Disney and, more than anything else, there were the movies and radio, especially the movies. I was looking at *Where the Wild Things Are* not too long ago with a friend, who had found something which amused her a good deal. She opened to one page of the book, where one of the wild things is leaning out of the cave. And then she held alongside it a still from *King Kong*, and it was practically a duplicate. But I had never seen the still, of course. Obviously, that moment had impressed itself on my brain, and there it was: the same proportions of cave to cliff, and of huge monster coming out of cave. It was extraordinary, the effect that movies had on me.

One critic has asked why you changed from the "fine engraved style" of Higglety Pigglety Pop! *back to what this person calls the "fat style" of your earlier work.*

Style, to me, is only a means to an end, and the more styles you have, the better. One should be able to junk a style very quickly. I think one of the worst things that can happen to young illustrators in art school is the tremendous focusing on "style," on preparation for coming out into the world of publishing and meeting the great, horned monsters, book editors. And how to take them on. Style seems to be one of the tricks. It's a great mistake. To get trapped in a style is to lose all flexibility, and I have tried very hard to prevent that from happening to me. I worked up an elaborate pen-and-ink style for *Higglety*. But I can abandon that for a felt-tip pen, as I did in *Night Kitchen*, and just go back to broadly outlined drawings with flat color. Each book demands an individual stylistic approach. If you have only one style, then you're going to do the same book over and over, which is, of course, pretty dull. Lots of styles permit you to walk in and out of books. So my point is to have a fine style, a fat style, a fairly slim style, and a really rough style.

Do you think of your books first in words or in pictures?

In words. In fact, I don't think of the pictures at all. Sometimes after I've written something I find that there are things in my story that I don't draw well. And if it were any other person's book, I'd consider not doing it. But I've written it and I'm stuck with it, which is proof to me that I have not (at least consciously) been seduced by the tale's graphic potential. If I'm stuck with buildings or an airplane, I might just manage. But an automobile means I'm ready to blow my brains out.

Do you think that children's book publishing is significantly different today than it was when you began in the early fifties?

Well, yes, of course, it's very different. For one thing, the world seemed quieter then, and there was more opportunity to do experimental kinds of books. If you're an artist, you must have the time to grow slowly and not feel pushed. It was that way in the early fifties. One could develop gradually. Now, of course, publishing is much more competitive, and we do many more books, but not many more good books. Something is lost. There is a rush, we are flooded with books, books come pouring out of the publishing meat grinder. And the quality has dropped severely. We may be able to print a book better, but are all the books being published worth printing? We have a backlist of books, superb books, by Margaret Wise Brown, by Ruth Krauss, by lots of people. I'd much rather we just took a year off, a moratorium: no more books. For a year, maybe two—just stop publishing. And get those old books back, let the children have them! Books don't go out of fashion with children. They just go out of fashion with adults and publishers.

[*1971*]

Really Rosie

My relationship with Rosie, the heroine of *Really Rosie*, began twenty-seven years ago. My earliest reference to her appears in a tattered, home-made sketchbook titled *Brooklyn Kids, Aug. 1948*. I was twenty and she was ten. We never officially met; once, however, when we passed on the street, she saluted me with a "Hi, Johnson!" Bewildering, but typically Rosie. She'd made me up on the spot. I don't recall her taking any further notice of me, though she must have been aware of the pasty-faced youth (me) watching from a second-floor window.

It seems, on the evidence of that sketchbook and the ones that came quickly after, that the better part of my day was spent at that window, Rosie-watching. The books are jammed with drawings of Rosie, her family and friends, and—along the sides of the pages—frantically jotted bits of precious Rosie monologue. My Rosie fever passed, so far as the sketchbooks are concerned, within nine months. One of the last sketches is captioned "Easter Sunday, April 1949" and depicts a very glum Rosie awkwardly arranged for church.

Who was Rosie and what was she to me? I was out of a job, out of sorts and money, and (worse) had to live at home with my parents, without a clue as to what to do next. Rosie occupied both hand and head during that long, languishing time and filled my notebooks with ideas that later found their way into every one of my books. Rosie was a fierce child who impressed me with her ability to imagine herself into being anything she wanted to be, anywhere in or out of the world. She literally forced her fantasies on her more stolid, less driven friends, and the tremendous energy she put into these dream games probably activated my own creativity. Her games were based mostly on the movies. She managed both the Charles Laughton and the Maureen O'Hara roles in *The Hunchback of Notre Dame*—one of her finest performances.

I became absorbed in the lives of the children across the street. I recorded their delight in the blizzard of December 1948, the well-attended first appearance outdoors of Rosie's new brother (she looks particularly piqued in these sketches), and a fantastic battle between her mother and her grandfather on the front stoop. There is Rosie cheering them on and giving a blow-by-blow description to the entire world via a make-believe radio microphone. These early, unprecise, wavery sketches are filled with a happy vitality that was nowhere else in my life at the time. They add up to the first rough delineation of the child all my future characters would be modeled on. I loved Rosie. She knew how to get through a day. A page filled with fat, snowsuited kids is punctuated, as always, with her familiar form. There is Rosie, the living thread, the connecting link between me in my window and the outside over there.

I did, finally, get outside over there. In 1956, after illustrating some dozen books by various writers, I did a Rosie and wrote my own. It is called *Kenny's*

Window and in it I paid homage to Rosie's street and house. *Very Far Away*, a year later, again takes place on Rosie's street, and the hero, Martin, acquired some of her aggressive personality. In 1960 Rosie made her official debut in my third book, *The Sign on Rosie's Door*. The events described in that book were culled and reworked from my 1948 sketchbooks; two episodes actually occurred and a lot of the dialogue is original Rosie. She had lost none of her luster and fascination over the twelve intervening years. My *Nutshell Library*, two years later, is intricately tied to *The Sign on Rosie's Door*. Alligator, Pierre, Johnny, and the nameless hero of *Chicken Soup with Rice* are modeled on the "men" in Rosie's life; the originals, in fact, appear in *Rosie's Door* under their proper names. Pierre, perhaps, is the most typical of all my published children—he could be Rosie playing Pierre! —and it was only a short step from Pierre to Max of *Where the Wild Things Are*. A mere change of sex cannot disguise the essential Rosieness of my heroes. I was not, however, finished with the real Rosie.

I have long wanted to make an animated film. This particular form is a deep old love of mine—beginning, as it does for all thirties children, with Walt Disney— and the influence of animation and flip-book techniques is plain even in my earliest work. The power of the early Disney shorts, their dazzling impetuosity, guaranteed their claim as a new art form, and the claim survived the test of Disney's first full-length animated features. It is easy now to scorn Disney's famous poor taste, but no creator of animated films since has matched his dramatic gifts. If anything, the anxious emphasis on so-called good taste enfeebles and ultimately drains the dramatic energy from most contemporary animation (I refer here to animation done with integrity, not the dread hokum of Saturday-morning TV). *Pinocchio*, my favorite of the full-length Disneys, is a passionate film, shrewdly paced, overwhelmingly inventive. There are flaws (Cleo's fluttering eyelashes and the pallid, unctuous Blue Fairy, for example), but the emotional conviction of the drama far outweighs them. Most important, Disney took maximum advantage of his medium. It is incredible, considering the labor, time, and expense involved, how exacting he was. There is, alas, no longer the money to fund such films; animation has become too costly a process. The cheating, short-shrift "animation" seen too often on television today—the dull, static figures merely moving their mouths or a finger or a foot, or blinking ad nauseam—is clear evidence of this. But there is no excuse for shallow content or lack of imagination or dishonesty. A slick surface does much to mitigate financial limitations and to deceive the eye, but, ironically, it draws attention to the emptiness below the surface.

When Sheldon Riss, an independent producer, approached me four years ago, suggesting I work with him on an animated film for television, I was anything but enthusiastic. Not only was I scornful of animated TV specials (they were never special), I had learned, through the punishing experiences of friends, to dread the networks. In the world of book publishing, I have command over my work—how it is printed and presented. I have earned that privilege and I am proud of it. I feared losing it in the world of despotic networks, among the vast crew of collaborators necessary for such a project. I held out for two years. Happily, so did Riss. There was no clink of coin in his enthusiasm, and his excitement and optimism finally won me over.

Once I'd committed myself to conceiving an animated film, I decided to play it safe and stick to what

I know best: those hurdy-gurdy, fantasy-plagued Brooklyn kids. My scenario, which incorporates the four books of the *Nutshell Library*, is about the ability of these children to overcome the tedium of a long summer's day and enforced imprisonment on an ordinary block. (You were never allowed to cross the street, walk in the gutter, or come upstairs except at mealtime or to go to the bathroom or to stop profuse bleeding. Food and other necessaries were dropped out the window, and street fights were screechingly arbitrated by mamas in adjacent windows.) It is no surprise that Rosie became the drama's connecting tissue, the point of it all.

Of course I overwrote, forgetting the limitation of twenty-four minutes of showtime for a half-hour feature. At one point, my scenario's bulk might have been mistaken for an adaptation of *The Don Flows Home to the Sea*. Carole King's score clarified everything. The seven songs she composed and performed (the four *Nutshell* texts, plus three new lyrics for Rosie) set the color and shape of the show; their length told me exactly how much script I had to cut. Rosie was finally becoming *Really Rosie*.

I embarked on a wild and woolly year as apprentice animator and director. I painted backgrounds and had the pleasure of rendering hundreds of drawings of Rosie and her gang that became the film's storyboard. Though *Really Rosie* was exhaustively delineated on paper, it took on a life of its own up there on the screen. The necessity of copying my style seemed not to shackle the animators; the staff of D&R Productions managed to get their own idiosyncrasies into the work, and *Rosie* benefited.

It became, oddly, coincidentally, a Brooklyn project. Carole King, Sheldon Riss, and I had all grown up in roughly the same neighborhood. I revisited it in order to refresh my memories, and Rosie's street—*my* street —brought back the boredom and loneliness of my time there. It was an ugly, bleak street. Rosie's old house was a nightmare of brand-new siding. I decided right then to move the setting of *Really Rosie* to another block. Every third year my sister, brother, and I had acquired a new apartment-street-school-neighbor-hood, for my mother loathed the chaos and stink created by housepainters—and in those faraway, dim days they *did* paint every third year. As a result, I had my choice of many streets. I decided to set *Rosie* on the shortest and best of them, only four blocks away from her real street.

We began this project with some heroic ambitions in tow. First, to create something that satisfied us. I had no desire to contribute to television yet another ersatz, ground-out kiddie thing. We vowed to pay attention to detail, we concentrated on content, and we let the form of the show evolve naturally—as naturally, I hoped, as children playing in the street.

It is immensely right that Rosie is the heroine of my first animated film. I believe in her now as firmly as I did twenty-seven years ago. She always did want to get into the movies.

[*1976*]

A Conversation with Walter Lorraine

WALTER LORRAINE: *How do you think an illustration functions in a book?*

MAURICE SENDAK: It's simply decoration or it's an expansion of the text. It's your version of the text as an illustrator, it's your interpretation. It's why you are an active partner in the book and not a mere echo of the author. To be an illustrator is to be a participant, someone who has something just as important to say as the writer of the book—occasionally something even more important.

Do you feel there are different categories of illustration?

Certainly, but I'll tell you only about the one I'm interested in and do well—interpretive illustration. It involves a kind of vigorous working with the writer. Sometimes you're the writer, too, so you're working with yourself; then the difficulty and strain and joy of that particular book is the balancing between the text and the pictures. You must not ever be doing the same thing, must not ever be illustrating exactly what you've written. You must leave a space in the text so the picture can do the work. Then you must come back with the word, and now the word does it best and the picture beats time.

It's a funny kind of juggling act. It takes a lot of technique, a lot of experience, to keep the rhythm going between word and picture. It's a kind of muscular rhythm, though the reader isn't aware of it. You have worked out a text that is so supple it stops and goes and stops and goes, and the pictures are shrewdly interspersed. The pictures become so supple, too, that quite independent of the words they tell their own side of the story.

The illustrator is doing a tremendous job of expansion, of collaboration, of illumination. But he must be discreet. The text should not intimidate him, but he must override his own ego for the sake of the story.

How would you define a picture book?

A picture book is not only what most people think it is—an easy thing to read to very small children, with a lot of pictures in it. For me, it is a damned difficult thing to do, very much like a complicated poetic form that requires absolute concentration and control. You have to be on top of the situation all the time to finally achieve something that effortless. A picture book has to have that incredible seamless look to it when it's finished. One stitch showing and you've lost the game. No other form of illustrating is so interesting to me.

Is there a particular style of writing that encourages a good picture book?

It can't be the pedantic sort of writing where every nail is knocked in. For my taste, it has to be ambiguous —it has to allow for a number of meanings to shine through. It can't be a heavyhanded text that says little Johnny goes from the left to the right, because then the illustrator doesn't have any choice but to make little Johnny go from the left to the right. The text has to be less precise, less obvious. You can have facts, but the facts have to allow the artist to move the characters in any direction.

Mother Goose is a good example. Many of the rhymes were probably conceived as social or political lampoons, but they have long since lost their original meaning. With "Hector Protector," for instance—a verse I've illustrated—you can make up your own story.

Hector Protector was dressed all in green,
Hector Protector was sent to the Queen.
The Queen did not like him, no more did the King,
So Hector Protector was sent back again.

Now what does that mean? Maybe a bit of a joke in Elizabeth I's day, but it means nothing to us now. However, it invites pictures. It's a very funny rhyme, the meter is lovely, and the language is peculiar. But what, for goodness' sake, is going on?—well, that's the illustrator's game. You have a nice little Mother Goose text that allows you to rearrange the characters in any way you like and make up a story, any story you want; it just has to spring from those words. Whatever tale you tell must begin with Hector Protector dressed all in green, but you can interpret that in new ways. He can be a boy in China, in Alaska, in Israel, but somehow or other he has to be dressed all in green. That's all you have to show. You can invent the rest. The whole book is your story as an illustrator.

How important is technique to the illustrator?
I think the better the illustrator is technically, the better off she or he will be—but it isn't essential. The peculiar gift in being an illustrator is that one has

an odd affinity with words, that it's natural to interpret words, almost like a composer thinking music when reading poetry.

Arthur Hughes is one of my favorite illustrators, but he couldn't draw people in three-quarter view! He worked from models, and so it's baffling that he couldn't draw people in three-quarter view. Well, he couldn't. You can see how wooden they look, how awful—as if their noses have been chopped off. It doesn't take an inch away from *The Princess and the Goblin*—it doesn't take anything away at all. I notice it because I am a craftsman, but I wish I had his gift. It doesn't matter that he didn't have the prowess of a Norman Rockwell. (I don't mean to put Mr. Rockwell down, but that's not what Arthur Hughes is all about.)

Arthur Hughes was an interpretive illustrator. He used whatever technique and craft he had at hand. It's not necessary to do elaborate and refined drawings, because elaborate and refined drawings with fantastic technique don't mean a hill of beans if you're not a good illustrator. Now, I suppose as Arthur Hughes got older, he learned to draw better. But alas, he also became a weaker illustrator. The last pictures he did look more graphically polished but have nothing of the power of those earlier "clumsy" drawings.

I'm saying this clumsily, too, because it's so hard to put this into language. I've seen so many gifted people who were natural illustrators who didn't have technical facility, but to me they had a great treasure. They had what you can't learn. You can draw better by practicing, but you can never learn that other, intuitive quality.

What do you think of the quality of picture books today?
Well, I'll have to make a very generalized statement

because I don't see that many of them. Much of what I do see is bad, and I think the form of the picture book has been, in large part, debased. It is overused, it is overdressed, it is garish, it is vulgar, it is despoiled. Somehow we've forgotten along the way how difficult it is to make a good picture book. Why don't we look at the major works around? Why don't we look at the little books of William Nicholson, *The Pirate Twins* and *Clever Bill*, which are seemingly so simple they run through your fingers, you can't catch them fast enough. Most of the new picture books I've seen are predictable—overcolored, overtechniqued, and over-written. Very few have excited me. There are exceptions. Some of the young people I teach have a fresher, more vigorous approach to the form. They give me hope for the future.

Was there a time when, in your opinion, picture books were better than today?

Yes. Of course there was Wanda Gág. There's always *Millions of Cats*. And we did have a glorious period in the 1950s and 1960s. American illustrators were tremendously stimulated by work coming from abroad. Remember the fifties, when Hans Fischer's books were first published here and *Finders Keepers* by Will and Nicholas won the Caldecott? I remember my excitement when I first saw it. It had an international flavor, which was something new in American picture books. And there was Tomi Ungerer, and a lot of others just beginning. We suddenly began to look very European. It was the best thing that could have happened to us—we looked terrific!

Do you think there is a lack of talent in picture books today?

I did think that for a long time. But since I've been

teaching I know it's not true. I've had the pleasure of working with some very talented, even brilliant young people. And I can say without hesitation that a few of my best students are ready to be published. They have an ethical approach toward the picture book, a vital and serious approach; and it has made me realize that my original view that talent wasn't there was probably false.

If talent is around but nobody is using it, what *is* wrong? It seems to me that the system is at fault. If you speak to publishers, every one of them will say, "We're always looking for new people." Then why aren't they being published? I've had great difficulty in placing some of my gifted students. What's the risk? It seems to me that publishers are less ambitious than they used to be, in general less brave, less willing to take risks. If you say this aloud, you get the standard response: "But we *are* publishing young people." Well, where are they?

My suspicion is that publishers are afraid. In the old days they did take chances. Nothing's happening now. I'm nearly fifty and when I turn around, I see very few young people climbing up the mountain. When I was young, in the fifties, we were given all the encouragement in the world.

Do you think that critical reaction today encourages superior books?

No. There are exceptional publishers, and there are a few exceptional critics—some *very* few exceptional critics—who take the trouble to evaluate a children's book in an intelligent way. They're not burdened with boring, tedious attitudes, such as whether a book is good for kiddies or not good for kiddies. They take an overall view of it aesthetically. Does it stand up as a work of art?

Speaking from my own personal experience, I have not learned anything from reviews of my books. And I've rarely seen reviews of other people's books that I thought did justice to a book's special qualities. Yes, there are some intelligent reviewers out there who can distinguish between the real and the phony. They take the larger view and escape the fatal Kiddie-booklanditis that most reviewers suffer from. But they are exceptional, very exceptional. Too often, children's books are judged by whether they conform to well-meaning but misguided rules about what children ought or ought not to be reading.

What do you mean by Kiddiebookland?
Kiddiebookland is where we live. Didn't you know? It's next to Neverneverville and Peterpanburg. It's that awful place that we've been squeezed into because we're children's book illustrators or children's book writers. Yes, we are! But isn't our work meant for everybody? How infuriating and insulting when a serious work is considered only a trifle for the nursery!

When you've worked a year on a book, when you've put your life into it, you expect the point of view of the professionals—editors, teachers, librarians—to be somewhat larger, more expansive.

Do you think critics should react differently to the illustrations in picture books?
I think they should try to learn what picture books are all about. There is some fine mystery in this difficult form, a mystery that is the artist's business. What I'm objecting to is that picture books are judged from a particular, pedantic point of view vis-à-vis their relation to children—and I insist that a picture book is much more.

When people review our books, a collision inevitably occurs with preconceptions concerning children. There is a standard theory about childhood that everybody works from, and critics check whether a picture book has followed the "rules" about what is right for children, or what is healthy for children, or what we *think* is right and healthy for children. This comes into conflict all the time with those things that are mysterious. Children are much more catholic in taste; will tolerate ambiguities, peculiarities, and things illogical; will take them into their unconscious and deal with them as best they can.

The anxiety comes from the adults who feel that the book has to conform to some set ritual of ideas about childhood, and unless this conforming takes place, they are ill at ease. An unavoidable conflict occurs because the artist cannot go by any specified rules. The artist has to be a little bit bewildering and a little bit wild and a little bit disorderly. That's the art of being an artist. Artists run into difficulty because they're dealing with our most upright, uptight business, which is the industry called childhood.

Most people are out to protect children from what they think is dangerous. Serious artists have the same concern. Their work, however, may not conform to what the specialists think is right or wrong for children. The artists are going to put elements into their work that come from their deepest selves. They draw on a peculiar vein of childhood that is always open and alive. That is their particular gift. They understand that children know a lot more than people give them credit for. Children are willing to deal with many dubious subjects that grownups think they shouldn't know about.

If a book doesn't follow the course of what a childhood specialist considers right, then it's a bad book for children. So picture-book people are more easily condemned than almost any other artists in creation because we're dealing with such a volatile subject—children. We must protect the children, and yet children are unprotected in every other way. No one protects them from terrible television. No one protects them from life because you cannot protect them from life, and all we're trying to do in a serious work is to tell them about life. What's wrong with that? They know about it anyway.

What should we look for in a picture book?
Originality of vision. Someone who has something to say and a fresh way of saying it. Do not look for pyrotechnics, for someone who can make a big slam-bang picture book out of very little. Look for the artist who thinks idiosyncratically.

Can you define what a picture book is for you?
Well, I think I have; it's everything. It's my battleground. It's where I express myself. It's where I consolidate my powers and put them together in what I hope is a legitimate, viable form that is meaningful to somebody else and not just to me. It's where I work. It's where I put down those fantasies that have been with me all my life, and where I give them a *form* that means something. I live inside the picture book; that's where I fight all my battles, and where I hope to win my wars.

[*1977*]

Laura Ingalls Wilder
Award Acceptance

Thank you. I'm so very pleased to be here. Many months ago I complained to my esteemed colleague and best friend Karla Kuskin that I could think of nothing more to say today than "Thank you. I'm so very pleased to be here." She shrewdly sized up the situation and guessed I was about to ask her help in editing my unwritten speech. After all, I sighed, what was there to say that would be new about Laura Ingalls Wilder or myself? Karla's reply was swift and typical: "Why don't you just tell them *Where the Wilder Things Are?*" Of course I was indignant. It was a bad pun . . . and I should have thought of it first. On the other hand, as an idea it had some possibilities.

But instead of telling you "where the Wilder things are," I am going to tell you about where they *were*. They were, in fact, in England in May of 1967. It was there that Laura Ingalls Wilder and I met under somewhat unusual circumstances. In northern England, Geordie country to be exact, I had a coronary thrombosis that spring and thus earned the dubious

[*This acceptance speech was given on June 28, 1983, at the meeting of the American Library Association in Los Angeles*]

distinction of being the only American at the Queen Elizabeth Hospital in Gateshead-on-Tyne, across the way from Newcastle. I was not quite thirty-nine, just beginning to understand the adage "Life begins at forty," when fate forced me to read the small print: "If you live that long."

On the morning of May 4, my friend and editor Judy Taylor and I journeyed by train up to Newcastle to enjoy the English countryside and to visit the studio of Thomas Bewick, the eighteenth-century engraver whose work I have always admired. As we approached our destination, I was appalled by the great ugly slag heaps that defaced the lovely spring landscape. I was tactless enough to mutter aloud at the desecration. Immediately, a portly gentleman sitting next to us slapped me on the back and said with good humor, "Young man, where there's muck, there's money." His statement has stayed with me ever since. It is an unhappy but near-perfect metaphor for the state of the arts . . . for the state of the world.

The day continued and seriously declined. I will spare you a re-creation of its more disastrous events. Suffice it to say that, after the official business of my coronary was settled and many bedridden weeks stretched before me, another crisis loomed. What to read? Judy and all my good friends rallied and in short order my room resembled a lending library. My memory of that coronary reading is vivid. Out of the dozens of volumes I consumed, there are a number that continue to hold a remarkably important place in my life. George Eliot's *Adam Bede* and all of George Eliot, J. R. Ackerley's *My Dog Tulip* and all of Ackerley, Philippa Pearce's *Tom's Midnight Garden* and all of the *Little House* books. I cannot say why I had a sudden longing to read Wilder, but I did and I communicated it to Ursula Nordstrom. Quickly and kindly she bundled the books into a Care package and sent them on. I devoured them like a starving man. Perhaps I needed the nourishment of something quintessentially American. Isolated by my illness in a cold, drizzly English world, I instinctively drew comfort and strength from that exemplary pioneer family to help me through my own troubles.

I want to quote from E. B. White's Wilder acceptance speech. Mrs. Wilder, he says, "behaved in a way that I find most admirable and enviable. Her prose has a natural simplicity and goodness that set it apart from the studied simplicity that often infects writing for children. In her books there are no traces of condescension—no patronage, no guile, and no cuteness. She speaks to us directly and brings her affectionate memories alive by the power of overwhelming detail and with a dramatic force that derives from honesty and accuracy." That, I think, eloquently sums up the virtues of Laura Ingalls Wilder as a person and an artist. Those virtues are embodied in her work as they are in much fine literature for children—in much fine literature. Calmly and clearly she illustrates the courage necessary to live an ordinary life. She is not concerned with fantasy heroics but with falling down and getting up, being ill and slowly recovering. What is important, she says, is to continue. In persevering, you will discover triumphs. This is what I was searching for, what I found in her books. I wanted to learn how to behave admirably in adversity, to be the kind of artist E. B. White praised so completely.

Not only did the *Little House* books establish themselves permanently in my heart; they have had, I suspect, no small influence on my work. And they left me, although it sounds impossible, with a happy coronary memory.

Three years after that dire English May, when I

came to write *In the Night Kitchen*, I filled it with graphic mementos and messages to the good doctors and nurses at the fine Queen Elizabeth Hospital in Gateshead, who had quite literally saved my life. Among the secretly noted thank-yous is one to Laura Ingalls Wilder. It manifests itself in Mickey's courage —and in my quest for the same, which I believe I owe in great part to the steadfastness and good humor of all the Wilders. In addition, there are the little houses which have been showing up in my work ever since that time. It cannot just be coincidence. There are little houses in *The Juniper Tree* and in *Some Swell Pup*. Last, and for me most significant, in *Outside Over There* the little house makes its appearance as the summer cottage just outside Vienna where Mozart finished his *Magic Flute*. The merging of those images—the sturdy little house and the artist I admire above all others in this world—expresses my feeling for Wilder things better than ten thousand words. I think you can appreciate, therefore, that this occasion is particularly sweet for me. My heart is pounding— now healthy and joyful. It joins me in thanking you for this special honor.

[*1983*]

Nutcracker

Could a ballet be a movie? Should a ballet be a movie? Didn't the requirements of one form violate those of the other? These disquieting questions occurred to me when the possibility of a *Nutcracker* movie finally became a certainty. They did not, however, shake my conviction that *Nutcracker* is the exception to every rule; it is not a proper ballet (ask any dancer) but rather a delightful mishmash of fairy tale, mime, and dance all threaded through with perhaps the best ballet score ever composed. Interpreters had to take liberties with it—historically, they always did. With the right director, there was every good reason to try to make a movie. And with Carroll Ballard committed to the project, we were in the best of hands.

Having already designed a stage production for Seattle, I was a seasoned *Nutcracker* veteran, and my eagerness to proceed yet again stood in odd contrast to my earlier indifference. Back in 1981, Kent Stowell, artistic director of Seattle's Pacific Northwest Ballet, had invited me to design the sets and costumes for a rigorously-faithful-to-Hoffmann-and-Tchaikovsky *Nutcracker*, which he would choreograph. Our 1982 production was well received, and we dearly loved "our baby."

My previous flip, disdainful attitude toward this work had yielded to a fascination that did not go away after opening night. *Nutcracker* was not the windy warhorse I had anticipated, and the sobering limitations of a proscenium stage only whetted my appetite for another go at it. How much more, technically and visually, a movie might achieve! In Carroll Ballard, we had a filmmaker who might bravely bite into the daunting old nut and prove yet again how versatile and full and fat was this tale by E. T. A. Hoffmann.

But Ballard also represented a potential danger. Weren't movie directors notoriously high-handed? Kent Stowell and I were possessive parents, and wouldn't that give Ballard misgivings? Would he listen to anything Kent and I had to say? If the three of us communicated and worked harmoniously together, couldn't we produce a shinier baby—a deeper and darker *Nutcracker*? But wasn't that about as likely as Clara's Christmas tree turning into a Chanukah bush?

In the beginning was E. T. A. Hoffmann; or so it seems natural to assume, considering his fairy tale "The Nutcracker and the Mouse King." But I would suggest a short step backward in time to Mozart, the adored hero of Hoffmann (who changed his middle name from Wilhelm to Amadeus) and Tchaikovsky's favorite composer, to whom he paid frequent homage. Mozart became the crucial element that fused together important aspects of the visual design and dramatic construction of the Pacific Northwest production of *Nutcracker*; even more so in my illustrated edition of Hoffmann's tale (blessed with Ralph Manheim's faithful and inspired translation); and finally, and most oddly, in Carroll Ballard's movie.

Before *Nutcracker*—before, in fact, any of his famous tales—Hoffmann was a composer of some accomplishment. Certainly *Undine*, his most celebrated work, is acknowledged as the first romantic opera, a link between Mozart, von Weber, and Wagner. It earned a favorable review from von Weber and even merited a letter of praise from Beethoven. Part of the score and all of the production were lost in a fire, and though Hoffmann intended to reconstruct the opera, he never did so. He became, instead, a great writer and, ironically, one of the most "composed to" of all writers.

While trying to decide whether I should design a production of *Nutcracker*, I took into consideration the image of Mozart that hovered over the work, and saw it as a good omen. But good omens do not good ballet productions make—at least, they are not to be counted on. And there was nothing in *Nutcracker*, other than the score, that interested me at first. Everything that made *Nutcracker* a traditional holiday delight—humongous Christmas tree and fatuous Candyland—depressed me. And what, heaven forbid, would *Nutcracker* be without them?

A good deal, Kent and I discovered, but we still had many minefields to cross. The first and most serious was the confusing fact that "in the beginning" was not Hoffmann at all but rather a French version of the tale, by Alexandre Dumas père. To make matters even more difficult, the scenario of the ballet is a pale hybrid based on Dumas and written in 1891 by Ivan Alexandrovitch Vsevolojsky, director of the Imperial Theater in St. Petersburg, and Marius Petipa, the choreographer, both of whom had been Tchaikovsky's collaborators on *The Sleeping Beauty*. Despite his own valid doubts about the scenario, Tchaikovsky proceeded to compose a score that sweeps Dumas aside and entirely restores Hoffmann. Tchaikovsky's music, bristling with implied action, is alive with wild child cries and belly rumbles. It does justice to the private world of children.

And that is the place where Kent and I found our *Nutcracker*. In that strange, uneasy light of half dream, half wakefulness that Clara inhabits. In the grave, often threatening, subterranean child's world that coexists inside the safe and happy house of Clara's parents. In the very parlor, in fact, where Clara's Christmas tree burns bright! It is a world familiar to all children, and it is this fidelity to child life that gives resonance to Hoffmann's tale and makes it an extraordinary work of art. The production of the ballet that Kent and I conceived was our effort to embrace Hoffmann—to get back to the gritty, slaphappy German Märchen that never quite explains itself but is fiercely true to a child's experience.

I met Carroll Ballard for the first time on January 20, 1986, in Los Angeles. My journal entry for that date is not encouraging: "I have met Lone Dog (that's the name of Ballard's production company) and he is Hoffmann's hard nut to the life. He is a diffident, opaque-faced man who mumbles and grunts, and who apparently doesn't want to make this movie. Why are we here?"

Carroll Ballard was famous (or infamous) for his extreme caution in attaching himself to projects, and his excitement over the Seattle production seemed to herald a great victory. It all seemed too good to be true. Alas, it was. My journal entries covering the five days of meetings in Los Angeles continue in lamentable fashion. The one for January 22 was typical: "C.B. is obtuse, stone-faced, and irritating beyond description. Why doesn't he just say no and go home!" Carroll "considered" for an inordinately long time. I was exasperated, and yet I had to sympathize. *Nutcracker* was a tar baby, something to avoid. Hadn't I felt the same way when I said no the first time around to Kent's proposal? How in the world resuscitate the tired old *Nutcracker* and turn it into something personal, vivid, and fresh, and yet faithful to its original source?

My journal entry for April 28 describes a meeting in Seattle to discuss the movie scenario for *Nutcracker*. Carroll had finally said yes. By April 30, my view of him had changed: "We are all adapting to Carroll's movie of *Nutcracker*. The basic outline is strong and good. Carroll is rough and subtle, open and shut. I like him." The actual shooting began on June 22, in Seattle, and though there are mutterings of "Carroll wafflings" in my journal, I was obviously more and more impressed.

Carroll, who fell in love with Clara and Drosselmeier, had, of course, to impose his own vision on *Nutcracker*. I was eager to see this, for I was now predisposed to believe in his vision. *The Black Stallion* and *Never Cry Wolf* (even more, some of his documentaries, which I finally got to see) gave me every reason to expect that this artist would find his own strong way into *Nutcracker*. In the meantime, I had to brace myself for the inevitable shocks, the manipulation and occasional dumping of what Kent and I had so painstakingly constructed for the stage—and all for cinematic reasons neither of us could comprehend. It became altogether a matter of trust.

Carroll often explained his reasons, and occasionally I even agreed. But sometimes decisions were made and important changes occurred before I *could* understand. So understanding didn't matter; mustn't matter. Trust was all, and trust I did. Besides, hadn't we fiddled and mustn't Carroll fiddle? He seriously fiddled and he took seriously our alarms and concerns. He went further, I suspect, than most movie directors would with fretful parents. But he never went so far as to placate us. I realized I could argue my point and lose my point without losing my respect and admiration for Carroll. I found myself relaxing and approving of my new role as apprentice to the director. I treasure the memory of his calling me over to "have a look" through the camera. I even had an opportunity to shoot a scene, and if this was a ploy for keeping me occupied and out of the way, it worked. Carroll may be taciturn, but he is the best—and shrewdest—of teachers.

What at first seemed only boring slowly became interestingly boring. I began to enjoy the new form—the new discipline—slow and wayward though it seemed. I began to catch the new and ponderous rhythm. And I began to absorb the shocks, sort of. My novicehood ended abruptly when the chandelier—my gorgeous chandelier!—was removed from the ball-room scene. I must have squawked loudly, for Carroll had it hauled down again and had me look at it through the camera's eye. It did clutter up the view, it did spoil the composition, it did get dumped. I felt chastened and almost resigned. I was in good hands.

I began to sense what a movie version according to Ballard must be like, what the stage production had to suffer to accomplish that feat, and how important it was for me to let go of the baby. A new collaboration was in the making. Fourth walls were hoisted up and painted; new *Nutcracker* nooks and crannies were ransacked; and lo and behold, a fresh point of view came into focus. Hoffmann's tale, like all the great Grimm Märchen, had many subtexts to uncover. Carroll found his own and it merged with the story

Kent and I told of Clara. It amplified and did justice to Hoffmann.

Superficially, Carroll and I couldn't be less alike. I hadn't read Peter Matthiessen (here Carroll registers quiet scorn for the out-of-it reader from the Big Apple). He loathed opera (I fume in Brooklyn hyperbole and denounce him for a lout). But since the movie was shot, I've read a Peter Matthiessen and he's seen an opera. Artistically, we have found common ground. We are both, it seems, interested in the small, quiet dilemmas of childhood; in the unspoken but deeply felt and often neglected pain of children; in the grave, uncomplaining nature of that pain or confusion, which is neglected not out of malice but rather because it is so quiet and uncomplaining; in the simple heroism of children and their touching efforts at concealment, as though to shield the grownups from too much pain.

Carroll still doesn't believe that Mozart's *Marriage of Figaro* is the most sublime of all masterpieces, and he still thinks *Amadeus*—the movie—was damned good entertainment. In fact, Carroll grew so tired of my Mozartian transports that he took his own peculiar revenge. In homage to my hero, I had placed a marble bust of him on top of the huge toy cabinet in the *Nutcracker* ballroom, a benevolent, beaming Mozart, looking down on all the Christmas proceedings with approval. (And why not? He's listening to a three-minute pastiche of himself, stolen from Tchaikovsky's opera *Pique Dame* and inserted into the ballet to serve our purposes.) During the transformation scene, while Clara was watching her familiar surroundings suddenly loom large and threatening, Carroll leaped onto his camera dolly with manic glee. He had the toy cabinet pushed toward the camera, and there, tottering on top, seen from a weird angle, was a terrifying Mozart, wobbling like a bogey man over poor Clara. Mozart the monster! I will always remember Carroll's malevolent cackle and glittering, wolfish eyes—his relish at my dismay, at my delight. Our friendship was sealed. After all, hadn't I found an original Lone Dog artist out of the land of the rich and famous—and wasn't that something of a miracle?

[1986]

An Informal Talk

I have been thinking lately about the monsters —or fantasies or whatever—that frightened me as a child, and that probably frightened me into being an artist. I can only come up with a few. My parents, of course. The vacuum cleaner, which still frightens me. My sister. A very few ordinary horrors from movies, books, the radio. The Lindbergh kidnapping. And, finally, school, for which I had a desperate loathing.

Aside from my parents—those occasional, and unwitting, monsters—the things that frightened me were mostly unpredictable, which goes to show that those people (myself included) who are determined to know what it is that scares children don't know at all. I think even a child psychologist would agree with that.

What interests me is what children do at a particular moment in their lives when there are no rules, no laws, when emotionally they don't know what is expected of them. In *Where the Wild Things Are*, Max gets mad. What do you do with getting mad?

[*This talk was given in Philadelphia in December 1985, under the sponsorship of the Rosenbach Museum and Library*]

Well, you're mean to your mother, and then you regret it, and then all becomes peaceful. It will happen again tomorrow, probably, but the problem for children, with their primitive logic and lack of experience, is passing from one critical moment to the next.

In my book *In the Night Kitchen*, Mickey's problem is: How do I stay up all night and see what grownups do, and have the fun that is denied me as a child? The fact that there was such an explosion when the book came out, that it could only appear in some libraries after someone painted diapers on the naked Mickey, seems to me grim testimony to our puritanical attitudes. Apparently, a little boy without his pajamas on was more terrifying to some people than any monster I ever invented.

Outside Over There is the most personal of my books, and my favorite. Much of it is based on what scared me when I was little. I remember as a very small child seeing a book about a little girl who is caught in a rainstorm. She's wearing a huge yellow slicker and boots, and the rain comes down harder and harder, and begins to rise and spill into her boots, and that's when I would always stop looking at the book. It scared me too much. I never found out what happened to the little girl. (Years later I thought I recognized her on the Morton saltshaker, and she looked okay. I mean, she got to be at least twelve years old.)

So *Outside Over There* is partly about that fear. It's also about Mozart, because I love Mozart and also because I was working on my first opera designs—for *The Magic Flute*—when I conceived this book. I set it in Mozart's time, in the last decade of the eighteenth century, the decade he died. So I was thinking of *The Magic Flute*, thinking of a little girl in a raincoat and boots, thinking of the end of the eighteenth century.

And I was also thinking of my sister, Natalie, who is nine years older than I am and who had to care for me. Today she's a very nice lady who lives in New Jersey and has no memory at all of the outrageous behavior that occurred between us. But I, alas, remember everything. It's one of the curses of my profession. I remember her demonic rages. I remember her losing me at the New York World's Fair of 1939. I also remember that she loved me very much. But my parents were both working hard and didn't have enough time, and so I was dumped on her. And that is the situation in *Outside Over There*: a baby is taken care of by an older child named Ida, who both loves and hates the newcomer.

There was a peculiar kind of baby boom in the early thirties. You had the Dionne quintuplets, you had Eddie Cantor dressing like a baby, and Baby Snooks, and, most important, you had the Lindbergh case. That is a memory all middle-aged Americans share, one of the most traumatic experiences of our lives. I remember it. I remember the headlines in the newspaper. I remember the anxiety. Lindbergh was the Prince Charles of his day, and his wife the Princess Di, and their baby a royal prince, a beautiful, blond, charming baby. At that time I was a very sickly child, and very worried about it, mainly because my parents were indiscreet enough to bewail my sickliness and carry on about how long I'd be around.

I learned early on that it was a very chancy business, being alive. Then this disaster occurred: an immaculate, rich baby, living on an estate, surrounded by warriors, you would think—German shepherds, guards, all the rest—on an ordinary evening, on an ordinary March day, this precious baby is taken away. I lived in terror and dread of what might happen to him. I remember Gabriel Heatter, the famous news commentator, reading the baby's formula over the radio, because the baby had a cold and Mrs. Lindbergh was worried about his being cared for.

Well, there I am, four years old, sick in bed and somehow confusing myself with this baby. I had the superstitious feeling that if he came back I'd be okay, too. Sadly, we all know the baby didn't come back. It left a peculiar mark on the mind.

All children—whether or not they grew up with the Lindbergh case—worry. Will Mama and Papa go away and never come back? Will I die? We don't like to think of kids worrying about such things, but of course they do. They have no choice, if they're intelligent and sensitive and alive to what's happening in the world.

In fairy tale and fantasy we reconstruct and defuse dreadful moments of childhood. *Outside Over There* became my exorcism of the Lindbergh case. In it, I am the Lindbergh baby and my sister saves me. It's Charlie Lindbergh brought back to life. And there is a reconciliation between Ida and her mother.

Ida's mother is not a monster. She is not indifferent to her children. She happens to miss her husband, and for one brief moment she leaves the baby. Even loving mamas turn away sometimes. You have to vacuum the floor, answer the telephone, go to your job, and just then kids are caught in a crisis—a very quiet crisis. You don't hear a scream, you don't hear a fall, but something occurs; and in the case of Ida, she has to make a quick decision. She is resentful about being stuck with the baby and flies into a rage, has a fantasy —a Lindbergh fantasy. But, finally, Ida restores everything to its natural order because, being a healthy child, she has to, she wants to. She loves the baby. She hates it only occasionally. In the end, the book is really a tribute to my sister, who is Ida, very brave,

very strong, very frightening, taking care of me. Baby.
I do care about children a lot. And when I say I
don't write for them, it doesn't mean I don't care for
them. I project into all my favorite music and pictures
an intense nostalgia for childhood, a passionate affilia-
tion with childhood. It's the same with literature—
from Melville to James, I always seem to find a sub-
text that involves children. Those are the reverberations that get to me and enter into my work.

I think some of the most touching moments in *The
Magic Flute* have to do with children. Much of the
opera focuses on the confusion of an adolescent girl.
Is her mother crazy? Is the man she loves crazy? Has
the solemn Sarastro saved her or kidnapped her? Isn't
this very much what life is like for many young people? Very arbitrary, no rhyme, no reason, no logic.
And then, when Pamina is about to commit suicide,
she is stopped by the three genies—as Mozart notes in
the score, *drei Knaben*, three little boys. When she has
lost all trust in all the adults in the opera, these three
kids say: "Don't do it, life is all right. He does love
you. Come with us and we'll show you." And they all
break into an incredible, happy quartet. The fact that
Mozart would give these boys the simple truth to
deliver reinforces my convictions about children and
their relationship to adults and the world.

Children are entirely at the mercy of adults—their
parents, their siblings, and their teachers. I suppose
there are the same kinds of dreadful people around in
schools today as there were when I was a child. I had
the bad luck to have several indifferent and unfeeling
teachers. But then I was a very difficult child. I hated
school. Even when I was encouraged to do what they
thought I wanted to do—write and paint pictures—I
had no pleasure, because I was doing it in a school-
room. So there was nothing that could be done for me.

My poor parents had to make countless trips to the school principal's office, and there were great mullings and puzzlings over how an apparently intelligent child could be so stupid all the time and so indifferent to what he ought to be learning.

The problem, so far as I was concerned, was to live until I was seventeen, so I could get out of school. It was just a matter of counting the years until then, when by law you could be free. The idea of college was anathema to me. The suggestion that you might choose to go on—total madness. So I didn't.

Our vacuum cleaner was surely the most eccentric of my childhood terrors. My mother would innocently bring it out—an old Hoover, the kind you plugged into the wall to make the bag swell up. So did I, apparently. They tell me I would start screaming uncontrollably at the sight of the vacuum, so I was allowed to go to the neighbors' apartment across the hall until the ordeal was over. I wonder why my mother never bought a quiet, compact model. Maybe it was too effective a weapon.

I used this fear when *Where the Wild Things Are* was turned into an opera some years ago. It's a book of only 385 words and it had to become an opera at least three-quarters of an hour long. So I amplified the opening scenes when Max gets mad at his mother. And to give this episode dramatic point, I had the mother enter with her vacuum cleaner, which drives Max bananas and which he then attacks with his sword. So this vacuum-cleaner phobia is now, to my astonishment, a significant moment in an opera.

At an early age, and for the sake of a set of dishes, I was taken to the movies every Friday night. If I'd been a Renaissance child and had lived in Rome, I could have gone down the block and seen Michelangelo working on the Sistine Chapel, and I would have been a much more enlightened and tasteful human being. But since I was a Brooklyn kid, there was only the Kingsway Theater, and you made shift. Occasionally, this looked-for pleasure scared me out of my wits. The offending movie, paradoxically, might be anything from Chaplin to Disney, and on one unforgettable evening we went to see *The Invisible Man.* Whenever it's on late-night television, I still try to watch it, without much success, because when Claude Rains unbandages his head and there's nothing there, it's Valium time for me.

These days I go to the movies once in a while. I was curious to see *Rambo* and took a young friend. Not only was I frightened, I was upset. I was surrounded by hysterically laughing children. I thought they were all crazy. But I finally realized that I was on a different wavelength completely, and what was very frightening to me didn't seem to frighten them at all. I've never heard so many chuckles and yucks every time somebody got blown up.

Maybe those old movies that scared me touched fears much closer to home. Children are always asking me where I got the idea for the Wild Things. I don't really know where they came from, but you have to tell children something. When I began drawing the pictures, I went the conventional route of griffins and other creatures from medieval iconography, which was very unsatisfying. Suddenly these characters began to appear and they were, surprisingly, people I knew.

I think it was the recollection of dreadful Sundays in Brooklyn when my sister, my brother, and I had to get dressed up for our aunts and uncles, none of whom I cared for particularly. I was an ungracious and ungenerous child, because what I really resented was that they were coming to eat our food. I never agreed for an instant that they should eat our food, or that we should share it. And I hated the fact that my mother was a very slow cooker, which meant that we had to spend what seemed like hours in the living room with people we detested.

We were, in other words, children. And the only relief from sitting and listening to the noxious "how big you've gotten" stuff was to examine those relatives critically and make note of every mole, every blood-shot eye, every hair curling out of every nostril, every blackened tooth. I lived in apprehension that, if my mother cooked too slowly and they were getting very hungry, they would lean over, pinch my cheek, and say, "You look so good, we could eat you up." And in fact we had no doubt they would. They ate anything in sight. And so, in the end, it seems that the Wild Things are those same aunts and uncles. May they rest in peace.

Despite the fact that I don't write with children in mind, I long ago discovered that they make the best audience. They certainly make the best critics. They are more candid and to the point than professional critics. Of course, almost anybody is. But when children love your book, it's "I love your book, thank you, I want to marry you when I grow up." Or it's "Dear Mr. Sendak: I hate your book. Hope you die soon. Cordially."

[*1987*]

Notes on
First Publication

THE SHAPE OF MUSIC : *Book Week, The Sunday Herald Tribune*, November 1, 1964.

MOTHER GOOSE : *Book Week, The Sunday Herald Tribune*, October 31, 1965.

RANDOLPH CALDECOTT : *The Randolph Caldecott Treasury*, edited by Elizabeth T. Billington (New York: Frederick Warne, 1978).

HANS CHRISTIAN ANDERSEN : *Book Week, The Sunday Herald Tribune*, March 13, 1966.

ADALBERT STIFTER : *Book Week, The Sunday Herald Tribune*, December 12, 1965.

GEORGE MACDONALD : *Book Week, The Washington Post*, July 24, 1966.

LOTHAR MEGGENDORFER : *The Publishing Archive of Lothar Meggendorfer* (New York: Justin G. Schiller, Ltd., 1975).

BEATRIX POTTER / 1 : *Publishers Weekly*, July 11, 1966.

BEATRIX POTTER / 2 : *Wilson Library Bulletin*, December 1965.

WINSOR MCCAY : *The New York Times Book Review*, November 25, 1973.

MAXFIELD PARRISH : *The Maxfield Parrish Poster Book* (New York: Harmony Books, 1974).

CLAUD LOVAT FRASER : *The Art of Claud Lovat Fraser*, edited by Clive E. Driver (Philadelphia: The Rosenbach Museum and Library, 1971).

JEAN DE BRUNHOFF : *Babar's Anniversary Album: Six Favorite Stories* by Jean and Laurent de Brunhoff (New York: Random House, 1981).

WALT DISNEY / 1 : *TV Guide*, November 11, 1978.

WALT DISNEY / 2 : *Book World, The Washington Post*, July 10, 1988.

EDWARD ARDIZZONE : *Book Week, The Sunday Herald Tribune*, February 6, 1966.

MARGARET WISE BROWN AND JEAN CHARLOT : *The Horn Book*, August 1955.

ERIK BLEGVAD : *Book Week, The Sunday Herald Tribune*, April 24, 1966.

Notes on First Publication

LOU MYERS: *Book Week, The Washington Post*, May 7, 1967.

TOMI UNGERER / HARRIET PINCUS / EDWARD ARDIZZONE / HARVE AND MARGOT ZEMACH: *Book Week, The Washington Post*, May 7, 1967.

ARTHUR YORINKS AND RICHARD EGIELSKI : *The New York Times Book Review*, December 10, 1978.

CALDECOTT MEDAL ACCEPTANCE: *The Horn Book*, August 1964.

BALSA WOOD AND FAIRY TALES: *McClurg's Book News*, January 1964.

FANTASY SKETCHES: *Maurice Sendak: Fantasy Sketches* (Philadelphia: The Rosenbach Museum and Library, 1970).

SOME OF MY PICTURES : *Pictures by Maurice Sendak* (New York: Harper & Row, 1971).

HANS CHRISTIAN ANDERSEN MEDAL ACCEPTANCE: *Publishers Weekly*, May 25, 1970.

A CONVERSATION WITH VIRGINIA HAVILAND: *The Quarterly Journal of the Library of Congress*, October 1971.

REALLY ROSIE : *Rolling Stone*, December 30, 1976.

A CONVERSATION WITH WALTER LORRAINE: *Wilson Library Bulletin*, October 1977.

LAURA INGALLS WILDER AWARD ACCEPTANCE : *Top of the News*, Summer 1983.

NUTCRACKER : *The New York Times*, November 23, 1986.

AN INFORMAL TALK : *The New York Times Book Review*, May 17, 1987.